Bank Job

About the Authors

James Heneghan was brought up in Liverpool, England, and in Ireland, where his parents came from. He was a police officer in Liverpool for a few years but decided to emigrate to Vancouver, British Columbia. After five years, he became a Canadian citizen. For twelve years, he worked as a fingerprint specialist with the Vancouver Police before deciding to become a teacher. He is now working with young people, teaching English at a high school.
James Heneghan is today one of the most acknowledged authors of historical fiction for children and young adults in Canada and the USA. Like "Bank Job", his award-winning books often tell stories of teenagers struggling to overcome personal difficulties.
He has won the Shelia A. Egoff Children's Literature Award three times for his titles "Flood", "Wish Me Luck" and "The Grave".

Norma Charles has written many books for kids, including "The Accomplice", which was short-listed for the Shelia A. Egoff Children's Literature Award. Like James Heneghan, she lives in Vancouver, British Columbia.
She worked as a librarian-teacher for over ten years before finally deciding to write full time. As the mother of four children — two boys and two girls — Norma Charles has had plenty of experience with children, and that experience has translated into her novels "The Accomplice" and "All the Way to Mexico", as well as several picture books.
She won the Coquitlam Pioneers first prize in 1989 for her short story "Lum King" and a British Columbia Book Award in 2000 for "Sophie Sea to Sea".
"Bank Job" was inspired by a real newspaper story of three teens who robbed seven banks in the Vancouver area.

James Heneghan & Norma Charles

Bank Job

Teen Readers · Teen Readers ·

TR

James Heneghan & Norma Charles
Bank Job
Teen Readers, level 2

Illustrations: Niels Roland

Editor: Charlotte Bistrup

ISBN Denmark 978-87-23-90768-4
www.easyreaders.eu

Easy Readers
EGMONT

Printed in Denmark

One

April 4

I told myself that a wet Tuesday afternoon was as good a time as any to *rob* a bank. Through the rain I was watching my friend Billy Galloway get ready to rob a Vancouver *branch* of the Bank of Montreal. Down the street in the *doorway* of Cameron's Shoes, my other friend Tom Okada was probably *cracking* his *knuckles* nervously while he waited.

I looked at my watch. 2:50 PM. My hands were *shaking*. I was waiting for Billy to give the signal. Billy is big with wide shoulders. He was wearing a blue baseball *c ap*, glasses, black *mustache* and a rain *jacket*. He pulled his cap forward in front of his face. That was the signal. Billy was going in. It was my turn to move.

I felt *sick*. I couldn't believe that I was doing this. I walked quickly into the bank and stood at a cash machine near the door. There were only two customers and two women *tellers* in the bank.

---

to rob to take money using force
branch [brɑːnʃ] local shop, office etc. belonging to a larger organization
doorway space in front of a door
to crack (here) the cause something to make a short, sharp sound
knuckle [ˈnʌkl] part of the finger where two of the small finger bones join
to shake – shook [ʃʊk] *– shaken* to move up and down very quickly and uncontrollably
cap, mustache [məˈstɑːʃ], *jacket* [ˈdʒækɪt], see illustration on page 9
sick ill or unwell
teller person who works in a bank giving money to or taking it from customers

Billy walked toward the younger of the two tellers and passed a note across the desk:

THIS IS A BANK ROBBERY. YOU WON'T GET *HURT* IF YOU DO WHAT I TELL YOU.

I knew what the note said because I had written it.

The teller reading the note wore glasses and looked like she was in her early twenties. Her hands were shaking as she pushed a *pile* of *bills* across to Billy.

I walked out into the rain and opened my shopping bag. Billy ran out of the bank and dropped his cap, glasses, mustache and the money into my bag. Then he ran round the *corner* of Tyne Street and was gone.

I walked quickly in the other direction. Tom Okada, waiting in the shop doorway, took my bag and put it into his *backpack*. He walked off in the direction of the *SkyTrain* station.

I stood in the shop doorway until I heard the police car coming. My legs were shaking so much that they could hardly hold me up. I tried to walk *calmly* along Kingsway toward the SkyTrain station. The police car passed me on its way to the bank. I looked at my watch: 3:05 PM. Lots of time, I told myself as I walked slowly on with a *thumping* heart. I wasn't carrying anything that linked me to the robbery. I was perfectly *safe*.

---

to hurt [hɜːt] – *hurt* – *hurt* to cause or feel pain
pile large number of things lying one on top of the next
bill *(AE)* banknote
corner, backpack see illustration on page 9
SkyTrain local railway system in Vancouver
calm [kɑːm] quiet; not showing strong emotion
to thump [θʌmp] to beat very hard
safe not at risk

There weren't many people on the street because of the rain, but the station was *busy*.

I got onto the train and fell onto the nearest seat.

I couldn't believe that the robbery would be so easy.

Eleven minutes later, at 3:16 PM, I got off at Patterson Station and by 3:32 PM I was back home.

'Home' was Janice and Joseph Hardy's old house on Oliver Avenue in Burnaby's Patterson Hill area. It was a *foster home*. Four kids lived at the Hardys'. First there was me, Nell Ford, thirteen. Most people called me Nails. Then there was Billy Galloway, now a real bank robber, fourteen. Tom Okada was thirteen like me. The fourth kid, Lisa Connors, had been at school, where Janice had a part-time job, during the robbery. She was nine.

Patterson Hill was a good place to live. Everyone was friendly. They knew that the green and white house on Oliver Avenue was a foster home.

The Hardys were not home from work yet. I took off my shoes and went up the *stairs*. Billy and Tom were waiting for me in their room. I walked in like a film star. I felt fine now. No one said anything until I'd closed the door.

"We did it!" I *cried* with a big *grin*.

"We did it!" cried Billy.

Tom was dancing on his bed like a *chimpanzee*. "We *friggin'* did it!" he cried.

---

busy ['bɪzi] a place where a lot of things are happening is a *busy* place
foster home home where children are looked after by adults who are not relatives
stairs [steəz] series of steps leading from one floor of a building to another
to cry *(here)* to talk in a loud, high voice
grin a wide smile
chimpanzee [ˌtʃɪmpæn'ziː] intelligent African monkey with no tail
friggin(g) this word is used instead of the rude word 'f***ing' to emphasize something

Tom got off his bed and put his arms around Billy's and my shoulders. We were the Three *Musketeers.*

"All for one and one for all!" we *chanted* as we did a *victory* dance between the beds. There wasn't much room. Finally we all fell onto Billy's bed, laughing.

"Show me the money," Billy said at last, sitting up.

I *emptied* the shopping bag onto Billy's bed and we counted the money. The total was $1,450. What a great success! Tom cracked his knuckles. We were over the moon.

The front door *slammed* and Janice called up the stairs. "Nell? Boys? Are you up there? Come and help me bring the shopping in from the car."

"Be right down!" Tom called back.

Billy put the money back in the bag. "We've got to hide this."

I *grabbed* the bag. "I've got a good safe place."

"Where is it?" asked Tom, cracking his knuckles *anxiously.* "We should know in case anything happens to you."

"Nothing's going to happen to me. Or to the money. We're all in this together. All for one and one for all!"

I carried the shopping bag to the room I shared with Lisa and closed the door.

You could easily see which side of the room was Lisa's:

---

musketeer [ˌmʌskəˈtɪə] soldier of the 17th century who carried a long, old-fashioned gun (musket); 'The Three Musketeers' is a novel by French author Alexandre Dumas
to chant [tʃɑːnt] to repeat words rhythmically
victory [ˈvɪktəri] a battle or a war which you have won is a *victory* for you
to empty [ˈempti] to take everything out of a bag, box, container etc.
to slam to close with force, causing a loud sound
to grab to take hold of something quickly and with force
anxious [ˈæŋkʃəs] worried

corner
jacket
backpack
cap
mustache

the *tidy* side with the pictures of cats and *kittens*. My side was the untidy side. I hardly ever made my bed. I didn't see the point. Lisa had a lot of books. I only had a few, but I loved to read and got books from the library.

I had recently read 'Pride and Prejudice' by Jane Austen. I loved all the *old-fashioned* language: words like '*amiable*' and '*agreeable*' that nobody uses today.

I liked Lisa a lot. I would say she is 'most amiable'. She is the closest thing to a sister that I will ever have.

I opened the *closet* and looked for the shoe box I'd been saving. Now I had the perfect use for it.

"Nell!" Lisa ran into the room. "Look what I've got!"

I jumped. I hadn't had time to *hide* the money. I pushed the bag under some clothes.

Lisa was holding a *tiny* orange kitten.

Her eyes were *bright* behind her glasses. "His name's Pumpkin. Isn't he beautiful? Feel how soft he is. Janice got him from someone at school. You can hold him if you like."

"Hey, you *guys*!" Janice *yelled* from below. "I said I need help down here with the shopping."

"Okay, we're coming," I yelled back. Then I said to Lisa,

---

tidy ['taɪdi] with everything in its right place
kitten baby cat
old-fashioned [ˌəʊld'fæʃnd] no longer modern
amiable ['eɪmiəbl] friendly and easy to like
agreeable [ə'griːəbl] pleasant
closet ['klɒzɪt] *(AE)* cupboard for keeping clothes in
to hide – hid – hidden to put something in a place where nobody can find it
tiny ['taɪni] very small
bright [braɪt] full of light and energy
guy [gaɪ] informal word for 'person'
to yell [jel] to call in a loud, high voice

"Show Pumpkin to the boys and tell them to go help Janice."

Lisa left. I pulled the shopping bag out again and put the money from the robbery into the shoe box. Then I grabbed a pen from my desk and wrote $1,450 on the *lid*. I felt inside the closet for the *loose floorboard*, pulled it up and dropped the box into my *secret* hiding place.

It was safe now.

I fell onto my bed and tried to *relax*. The emotional stress of the last few hours had *exhausted* me.

I *sighed*. What had I done? I was a bank robber. A real bank robber. I was a *criminal*.

So much had changed in only one month.

---

lid cover of a box, bottle, jar etc.
loose [luːs] not firmly in place
floorboard [ˈflɔːbɔːd] piece of wood from which a floor is made
secret [ˈsiːkrət] known only to a few people and hidden from all others
to relax [rɪˈlæks] to become quiet and calm again
to exhaust [ɪgˈzɔːst] to make a person very tired
to sigh [saɪ] to express sadness by letting air out of your mouth with a long, low sound
criminal [ˈkrɪmɪnəl] person who has broken the law

Two

March 2 – one month earlier

Our social worker's name was Rhoda Mills. She loved her work and was good at it. She visited us a couple of times a year and always remembered our names. She was in her thirties maybe, with brown hair and glasses that kept *sliding* down her nose.

It was just after four o'clock. Joseph had taken time off from work. It was an important meeting. We all had to be there.

Janice showed Rhoda our bedrooms (especially tidy for her visit). We kids stayed out of the way, and after a look at the bathroom (also especially tidy) the *grown-ups* came back down into the kitchen. Rhoda sat down at the table and Janice brought tea and *cookies*.

"How are things with you kids?" Rhoda asked, looking mainly at me. "Nell?"

"Things are good," I said.

"How's your mother?" asked Rhoda. "You still see her regularly?"

"Of course," I said. "Weekends, whenever I can. She's fine."

"Billy? Tom? Lisa? Anything new? You kids okay?"

---

to slide – slid – slid to move smoothly along a surface
grown-up ['grəʊnʌp] person over the age of 18
cookie ['kʊki] *(AE = American English)* biscuit

The other three smiled back and said it was all fine.

"Feel free to go, kids. Unless there's anything you want to talk about," said Rhoda "I need to talk with Janice and Joseph for a minute."

* * *

"It's *strange* to hear someone other than Janice or Joseph call you Nell," said Tom. All my friends called me Nails. "How did you get the *nickname* Nails anyway?"

"You really want to know?" I asked. "Well, it's a long story. I've lived in foster homes since I was a baby. Most were okay, but the one before I came here was *terrible*."

"Terrible?"

"Terrible. Are you *gonna* repeat everything I say?"

"Sorry."

"It was run by an old *cow* called Mrs. Osberg – the kids called her Iceberg – who hit us with a *cane*…"

"She hit you with…?"

"With a cane, yes. If you *interrupt* me once more…"

"Sorry. I'll *shut up*. I promise."

"She hit us if we did anything she didn't like. She was new to *fostering*, and we knew that if the social worker found

---

strange [streɪndʒ] unusual
nickname [ˈnɪkneɪm] a name – not the person's real one – given to a person by family or friends
terrible [ˈterɪbl] very, very bad
gonna (*AE*) going to
cow [kaʊ] 1. animal that gives us milk; 2. woman who is not nice
cane thin stick (usually bamboo) used in the old days to hit schoolchildren
to interrupt [ˌɪntəˈrʌpt] to break into what somebody is saying
to shut [ʃʌt] *up – shut – shut* to stop talking; to close (= shut) your mouth
fostering the activity of being a foster parent

out what was going on, that would be the end of her as a foster parent. She hit me with the cane a lot of times, but I never cried, and this made her *angry*. 'You're as hard as *nails*!' she said one day in front of the other kids. That's now I got my nickname. I rather liked it."

"It *suits* you," said Tom. "Nails are hard, but they're sharp and they're strong. Just like you."

Tom was a good listener, except when he interrupted. Billy didn't say anything, but I knew he was listening. So I went on with my story.

"One day, when Iceberg was hitting me for no good reason, I decided to live up to my new name. I *kicked* her on both *shins*. She fell down onto the floor, *screaming*. I ran out of the house. The police found me late that night. Social Services closed old Iceberg down and sent me here. I've been here ever since. That's the story."

"Wow!" said Tom. "What a story!"

* * *

Janice called us downstairs for a family meeting when Rhoda had gone. She and Joseph were sitting at the kitchen table looking *grim*.

---

angry ['æŋgri] full of strong emotions that make you want to shout at or hurt somebody
nail [neɪl] sharp piece of metal used to hold pieces of wood together
to suit somebody [suːt] to go well with a person's character or appearance
to kick to use your foot to hit something
shin front part of your leg just above your foot
to scream [skriːm] to call out loudly in pain or fear
grim looking or feeling very seriously worried or unhappy

"Kids," Janice said, "we've got some bad news."

"Is there a problem with Social Services?" I asked.

When I had first come to the Hardys' there had been a problem with the old-fashioned bedroom windows which wouldn't open. 'Kids need *fresh* air' the social worker had said. So Joseph had spent the weekend fixing them.

We sat. Joseph opened a bottle of *beer*. He wasn't a big man. Billy was a few *inches taller*, but Joseph looked firm and strong. Janice, sitting next to him, was a calm, motherly woman. They had got married as teenagers and still loved each other. They had wanted kids but it had never happened. We were their kids, their family.

Joseph sighed as he told us that there were new Social Services *regulations*. "One of the regulations is that with six people in the house, we need two full bathrooms. Two point five bathrooms would be ideal."

I looked at Billy. Billy looked at me. I knew what he was thinking. The Social Services were right. There was a full bathroom upstairs, but only a toilet and *sink* in a small room downstairs. So what? It was an old house.

"We *manage* okay," I said. "Usually, anyway."

"Not good enough," said Joseph. "We knew last year that there were going to be new rules, so we checked..."

"...with the Foster Parents Association," said Janice.

sink

fresh new and clean
beer [bɪə] popular drink containing a little alcohol
inch [ɪntʃ] unit of measurement = 2.54 cm
tall [tɔːl] high (of living creatures, buildings etc.)
regulation [ˌregjəˈleɪʃn] official rule
to manage [ˈmænɪdʒ] to be able to do something difficult

"And they couldn't help us," Joseph went on.
"The new regulations are here to stay," said Janice. "They've given us six months to *comply*."
"What does 'comply' mean?" asked Lisa.
"Right now, it means 'get another bathroom'."
I said, "What happens if we don't get one?"
"Social Services will reduce the number of kids we can look after..." said Joseph, looking *sadly* at Janice.
"...to one or two," Janice finished for him.
"What?" cried Tom. "Two of us would have to go?"
"Break up the family?" I cried.
"*I'm afraid so*, Nell," Janice said.
We all *groaned*. Not another *foster*, I thought. Not another move when everything was perfect here. Not when I'd finally found a family where I belonged.
"Friggin' Social Services!" said Tom.
"Don't *blame* Social Services," said Janice. "They only want what's best for kids."
Joseph said, "We've already thought about..."
"...*remodeling* the downstairs toilet," finished Janice.
"That's it," said Tom, looking at Billy. "No problem!"
"The only problem is money," said Joseph. "I asked a builder to price the work. He said it would cost..."
"...ten thousand dollars with everything." said Janice.

---

to comply [kəm'plaɪ] to do what the regulations tell you to do
sad unhappy
I'm afraid [ə'freɪd] *so* I'm sorry, but that's what will happen
to groan [grəʊn] to sigh loudly and with deep sadness
foster short for foster home or family
to blame somebody to say that somebody is the cause of something bad
to remodel [riː'mɒdəl] to change the shape or use of something

"Ten thousand dollars we don't have right now," said Joseph.

"So what you're saying," said Tom, "is that at least two of us will have to go and live somewhere else."

I looked at Billy and he looked at me. Tom was busy cracking his knuckles and Lisa was about to *cry*.

Janice said, "We've got six months to find a solution."

We *stared* at each other. Leave Janice and Joseph? *Deadly*. I knew how I felt and I knew how the others felt. No one wanted to leave the Hardys. I would do almost anything to stay. Anything.

Janice looked at all of us. "I don't want you to worry too much," she said. "Joseph and I..."

"We're going to do everything we can," said Joseph.

"We didn't want to worry you," said Janice. "But...

"...we don't want any *secrets* in this family," Joseph finished the sentence for her.

* * *

That night, when Janice came up to say goodnight to Lisa and me, she smiled at us even though she looked worried.

"I don't want you two to worry," she said. "I'm sure everything will work out."

---

to cry *(here)* to show a strong emotion of sadness by letting water come out of your eyes

to stare to look at somebody or something for a long time

deadly very serious; likely to cause death

secret [ˈsiːkrət] piece of information which you do not want people to know

"But what if it doesn't?" asked Lisa. "I don't want to leave here. You, Joseph and the others are my family."

"I know, *Sweetie Pie*," said Janice. "And we don't want to lose you either."

Lisa began to cry. I felt like crying, too. There had to be something we could do. We had to stay together.

Sweetie Pie [ˈswiːtiˌpaɪ] friendly way of addressing a girl or young woman you like or love

THREE

March 3

I got the idea for the Three Musketeers the next night while we were watching an old *movie* about three *loyal* seventeenth century soldiers of the king of France. The film was not as good as the book. I had read it, but the movie was full of action and made a change from the *gangster* films we usually watched.

Billy and Tom liked the Musketeers movie too. I loved their *slogan* 'All for one and one for all'. *Loyalty* and *friendship*. If only we could fight for Janice and Joseph and Lisa. And for ourselves, of course. We didn't want to break up the family, so why couldn't we try to raise the ten *grand* for the extra bathroom? The three of us, the Three Musketeers. Why not?

* * *

The next morning I was still thinking about the Three Musketeers while we were up early, doing our usual Saturday jobs around the house before breakfast.

---

movie ['mu:vi] 'moving' film shown in a cinema
loyal ['lɔɪəl] always ready to help your friends, family, king, country etc.
gangster ['gæŋstə] member of a group (gang) of violent criminals
slogan ['sləʊgən] motto; short phrase that describes a product, aim, belief etc.
loyalty ['lɔɪəlti] quality of staying loyal
friendship relationship between friends
grand slang word for 1000 dollars, pounds, euros etc.

Janice called us when breakfast was ready.

Janice and Joseph were unusually quiet. We were pretty quiet, too.

After breakfast, Janice took Lisa shopping and the boys and I went for a walk in the park. I could tell that Billy had a plan and I wanted to tell him about mine.

Patterson Hill Park was at the end of the *block*, not far from the house. We sat down at a *picnic* table – Billy sat on the table with his feet on the seat. Tom looked *impatiently* at Billy, but Billy was in no *hurry* to tell us about his plan. Finally he said, "What do you guys think we should do about this extra bathroom?"

"Huh? There's nothing we can do," said Tom. "Not as far as I can see. I agree with the regulations. One bathroom for six people isn't enough. I used to have my own bathroom. We had four in our house – for three people. Can you believe it? That was before my *mom* and dad..." He stopped.

Billy looked at Tom. "So you don't mind leaving the Hardys?"

Tom said nothing. But he turned away from us.

I said, "I know what we can do. We could be like the guys in that movie last night, the Three Musketeers, working together, all for one and one for all. We could go out and get what we need."

Tom turned angrily to me. "Ten thousand *bucks*? How can we raise that kind of money? *Babysitting*? Dog-walking?

---

block group of buildings between two parallel streets or the distance between them
picnic ['pɪknɪk] food that is taken to be eaten outside
impatient [ɪm'peɪʃənt] not able to wait for something
in a/no hurry ['hʌri] more/less quickly than usual
mom *(AE)* mum
buck *(AE slang)* dollar
babysitting looking after young children

Sometimes, Nails, I think you must be *crazy*."

But Billy didn't think I was crazy. "Nails is right. There **is** something we can do. I've got a plan."

"What kind of plan?" asked Tom.

"The only way we're gonna get that sort of money..." he looked first at Tom, then at me, "is to *steal* it."

"What?" cried Tom, *shocked*.

"Very *funny*," I said, but I wasn't laughing.

"I'm serious," said Billy. "We need to be like the Three Musketeers. They stole from the bad guys and gave to the good guys. Nails is right. We need to go out and take what we need."

"You're thinking about Robin Hood," said Tom. "The Three Musketeers didn't steal. They protected the king."

"Well, we would be protecting the family," Billy said before I could open my mouth. "Same thing."

"Stealing is for losers," said Tom. "We all know that."

"Who were you thinking of stealing from?" I asked.

"The bank," said Billy. "That's where the money is."

For once, Tom was *speechless*. So Billy went on.

"Think of Joseph's old gangster movies. Think how easy it is! You walk in, you tell them it's a *holdup*, and you walk out with their money."

"But you need a *gun* or a *knife*," I said.

"In some movies the robbers only have a note – not guns or knives," said Billy.

"You're crazy. You'd never get away with it," said Tom.

---

crazy ['kreɪzi] mad; not very sensible or intelligent
to steal – stole – stolen to rob; to take money etc. without permission
to shock somebody to give somebody a very unpleasant surprise
funny ['fʌni] something which makes people laugh is *funny*
speechless ['spi:tʃləs] so surprised that you cannot speak
holdup ['həʊldʌp] robbery

gun [gʌn]

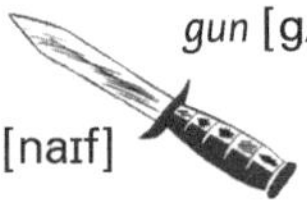
knife [naɪf]

"Bank robbers get caught and go to *prison*."

"Not if they work together like *pickpockets*."

"What have pickpockets got to do with it?" I asked.

"A pickpocket is *smart*," he said, turning to me. "As soon as he steals something, he gives it to a partner as quickly as he can. So if the victim or the police grab the pickpocket, they find nothing on him. We would do the same thing. It's simple. We could raise the ten grand in no time. Don't you see?"

"No way," Tom shook his head. "I don't want to hear any more." And he started walking away from us.

"Come back and talk!" Billy called after him.

Tom stopped. I could see he was trying to decide what to do. Finally he came back, but he was not *convinced*.

Nor was I. "Tom's right, Billy," I said. "It's nice of you to think of a way to keep us together, but kids robbing banks makes no sense. No sense at all."

Billy just smiled, and when Billy smiled at me like that, I would do anything for him. As Jane Austen would say, Billy was a very amiable young man.

Then he smiled at Tom as well.

Tom *shrugged* and looked down at his shoes. "Sometimes, Billy," he said quietly, "I think you should be in a *mental* hospital, not in a nice place like the Hardys'."

Billy laughed and put an arm round Tom's shoulders. We all walked back to the house together.

---

prison ['prɪzn] place where criminals are sent for punishment
pickpocket ['pɪkˌpɒkɪt] person who steals things out of people's pockets
smart *(here)* intelligent
to convince [kən'vɪns] to show somebody that your idea or opinion is correct
to shrug [ʃrʌg] to move both shoulders up and down to show that you do not know something or care about something
mental ['mentl] connected with the mind

FOUR

March 11

A week had gone by, and we still hadn't thought of a better plan to raise the money.

Billy tried to *talk us into* his crazy bank-robbery idea again, but we told him to shut up. His smiles weren't working.

I thought that Mom might be able to help.

My mom is Carolina Ford. She lives less than an hour away in an apartment on False Creek, Vancouver. So I went to visit her. On the way, I thought about money.

Billy wanted us to rob banks. Tom *hated* the idea. It was *dangerous*. If my idea worked out, we wouldn't need to steal.

I got off the SkyTrain at Granville Station and took a bus to False Creek. My mom's small apartment is on Commodore Road. I opened the door with my own *key*. Mom was watching TV in her *bathrobe*, as usual, with a can of Coke in her hand, also as usual.

Zero activity and sweet drinks were making her *fat*.

"Hi, Mom. How are things? Did you remember to eat breakfast?"

---

to talk somebody into something to convince somebody that something is a good idea

to hate opposite of 'to love'

dangerous [ˈdeɪndʒərəs] involving very great risks

key [kiː] piece of metal that can open a locked door

bathrobe loose piece of clothing that you put on after having a bath or shower

zero [ˈzɪərəʊ] the number '0'

fat having too much body weight

The apartment was in a *mess*, like my half of the room at home. Maybe I was like Mom in some ways.

My mom is mentally *handicapped*.

I sometimes think I must be mentally handicapped, too. I'm hopeless at school except for English. I'll be happy when I can leave school and find a job.

Mom's got the mind of a child. She can only look after herself with help from Social Services. But she's sweet and always happy.

I sat beside her on the sofa and gave her a big *hug*. She hugged me back.

"I'll *scramble* some eggs. Your *favorite*. Would you like that? Scrambled eggs on toast?"

Mom watched TV most of the day.

"Don't worry about breakfast, Sweetie," said Mom. "I'm not *hungry*."

"That's because of that sugar water you're drinking. After breakfast, I'll do your hair. Would you like that?"

She raised her hands to her thick, dark hair. It was in a mess. "Oh, would you, Nell? I'd like that a lot."

Mom was almost forty. When she was twenty-four she had married John Ford, also mentally handicapped. Then

---

mess very untidy state
handicapped ['hændɪkæpt] physically or mentally below the normal standard
hug [hʌg] when you hold somebody tightly in your arms you are giving them a *hug*
to scramble ['skræmbl] to mix together (parts of an egg) and then fry, moving the mixture all the time
favorite ['feɪvrət] *(AE spelling)* the thing or person you like best is your *favo(u)rite* thing or person
hungry ['hʌŋri] wanting food

they had me, their first and only child. My father was working at a *gas station* at the time.

I was taken away from them after only a month. They were *incompetent* parents. The Social Services tried to help, but I was left unwashed and *unfed* for hours while my mother watched TV. Finally, the neighbors called the police.

How do I know all this? I read the newspaper story years later. The paper said that the new baby (me) was at risk and should be 'removed to a place of safety'. The experts said the new baby was 'normal', but I've never believed that. I mean, how can two mentally handicapped people have a normal baby?

There was a *court hearing*. The judge decided that Baby Nell (me) could not stay with her parents. My mother cried all through the hearing. All she knew was that they were taking her baby away from her.

The headline of the article was: *TRAGEDY* WITHOUT *EVIL* – *RETARDED* PAIR LOSES BABY.

No one says 'retarded' now. Now they say 'mentally handicapped' or '*intellectually challenged*'. I've read that story many times. I know every word of it. It was a long time before I could even look at it without crying.

---

gas station place where petrol (*AE* 'gas(oline)') is sold to motorists
incompetent [ɪn'kɒmpɪtənt] very unable to so something properly
unfed [ʌn'fed] not given food
court hearing meeting with a judge in a court to decide an important matter
tragedy ['trædʒədi] very sad event
evil ['iːvəl] very bad or wrong situation or action
retarded [rɪ'tɑːdɪd] held back in its development
intellectually challenged [ˌɪntə'lectjʊəli‿'tʃælɪndʒd] finding it difficult to learn things

* * *

Mom was talking to me. Something about her hair.

"Sorry, Mom. Was I pulling it? So dark and thick! It's easy to see where I get my hair from."

"And your lovely green eyes, Nell. You get your eyes from me, too. Don't forget your lovely green eyes."

She relaxed as I *brushed* her hair.

"Mom, could I ask you about your *pearl necklace.*"

Mom thought for a while. "The beautiful pearl necklace my mother left me?"

"Yes. Will it be mine some day?"

"Of course it will, Sweetie. And my music box. And my book of stickers from *Expo 86*. And my picture of your daddy at the gas station in his *smart uniform* a month before he died. Everything will be yours."

"Could I see the necklace?"

"See it now?" Mom looked *confused*. Had she forgotten where it was? "Is my hair finished?"

"Come over here and look at it. It looks great!"

* * *

to brush [brʌʃ] to use a *brush*

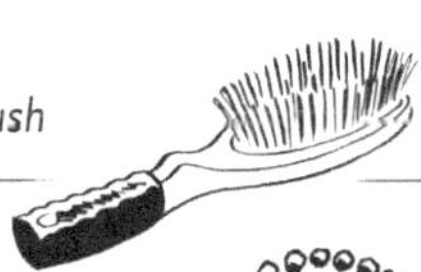

Expo 86 transport and communication exhibition (exposition) held in Vancouver in 1986

smart (here) looking good while wearing attractive, tidy clothes

uniform [ˈjuːnɪfɔːm] clothes worn by members of a group (army, police, railway staff etc.) to show that they are members of the group

to confuse [kənˈfjuːz] to make somebody unsure of what is happening

pearl necklace [pəːl‿ˈnekləs]

On the SkyTrain home I took Mom's necklace out of my jeans *pocket* and looked at the beautiful pearls. She wouldn't *miss* it. I hadn't taken the box. And even if she opened the box and saw it was *empty*, she wouldn't remember showing me the necklace. And anyway, it was really mine. She was going to give it to me one day.

I got off at Metrotown Station and ten minutes later I was showing my necklace to a man in a *jewelry* shop.

"How much is it worth?"

He just smiled at me. "It's *costume jewelry*. They're not real pearls. I'm sorry," he said, "but this is worth very little. Thirty dollars maybe. Certainly no more than fifty."

Fifty dollars! I put the pearls back into my pocket.

"Thanks very much," I said, and walked quickly out of the shop, expecting to hear the shop man laughing at me, the mentally retarded kid.

jewelry [ˈdʒuːəlri]
(*BE spelling:* jewellery)

pocket small bag on the inside of a piece of clothing
to miss something (here) to find out that something is no longer in its right place
empty with nothing inside it
costume [ˈkɒstjuːm] *jewelry* jewellery that is not made of real gold, real jewels etc.

Five

March 12

The next afternoon we got together around our usual picnic table in the park. The wind was shaking the heads of the yellow *daffodils* from side to side as if they were saying 'No! No!' That should have told me something.

"You have to go into the bank, Billy," I said, "and give the bank teller the note. You're the biggest. You look about eighteen, maybe nineteen."

Billy had convinced me that the only way to get so much cash was to go along with his robbery plan.

"You could get the money," I said, "run out of the bank and Tom would be waiting..."

"No friggin' way! Look – I've got a better idea. There's a *trust fund* been set up for me for when I'm older. Maybe I could get my hands on some of it."

I felt like hugging him. "Oh, Tom, that'd be so wonderful." I turned to Billy. "Wouldn't it, Billy?"

Billy looked *disappointed*. "Yeah. Sure it would."

* * *

---

daffodil ['dæfədɪl] →
trust fund ['trʌst‿fʌnd] money belonging to somebody which is looked after until that person reaches a certain age
disappointed [ˌdɪsə'pɔɪntɪd] unhappy because something you wanted to happen has not happened

Billy waited a few days before asking Tom about the money. We were on our way home from school.

"Well? Did you get it?"

Tom looked away from us. He said nothing for a while. Then he said, "Couldn't get it. There's money for university but nothing else. Not until I'm twenty-one."

I could see that Billy was trying not to look *pleased*.

* * *

The next Saturday was cold and windy. We were sitting at our usual picnic table in Patterson Hill Park.

"So what's it to be, Tom?" asked Billy.

"If you're talking about robbing banks, my answer's 'no'."

Billy turned to me. "So it's just you and me, Nails."

I shrugged. Billy came over and sat beside me with his back to Tom.

"So it's back to my plan. I do the holdup, okay?"

"Okay," I said, "and you pass the money to me. Do you think it will work, Billy? You think we can do it?"

Billy smiled. "*Trust* me. I don't see how it can fail."

Billy filled me with hope, and I trusted him. We would get the money for the extra bathroom. No one would have to leave the Hardy home at all. I told Tom that we needed his help. "If there's three of us, we'll be like the Three Musketeers. All for one and one for all."

Tom shook his head. "Friggin' *stupid* I call it."

---

pleased [ˈpliːzd] very happy that something has or has not happened
to trust somebody to believe that somebody will not leave you in a risky situation
stupid [ˈstjuːpɪd] not very intelligent

He shouldn't have said that! I turned to Billy. "Okay, Billy. It's just you and me. So I'm standing there with the bag of money. Now what do I do?"

But Billy had not given up on Tom. "It would be safer to have a second *handoff*, Tom. We really need you."

Tom shook his head, but I could see how much it hurt him to say 'no' to Billy. There was *silence*, so I repeated my question. "So I'm standing there with the bag of money. What do I do next?"

"You walk down the street to where Tom is waiting."

I said, "But Tom..."

"Don't worry. Tom will change his mind. He won't *let us down*. You give the bag to Tom and we go home by different SkyTrains. We mustn't be seen together."

No one but his best friends, us, could know that quiet, *sleepy*-looking Billy was a *pirate* at heart.

"I'm with you, Billy," I said, "if it means keeping the four of us together at the Hardys'."

"I knew I could count on you, Nails," smiled Billy.

When he said things like that, I felt warm inside.

Tom was quiet on the way home. So I talked to Billy.

"You must be six foot tall. You look like a bank robber from the back. Like the one in that old black-and-white western movie we saw. I forget his name..."

---

handoff action of giving something to somebody quickly
silence ['saɪləns] lack of any kind of sound
to let somebody down to not help somebody when you know they need help
sleepy ['sliːpi] *(here)* showing very slow, calm reactions
pirate ['paɪrət] criminal seaman who uses his ship to steal from other ships

Billy smiled. "You mean Billy the Kid? Yeah!"

"But you need a *disguise* to look older," I went on. "From the front you really do still look a bit like a kid!"

Billy said, "Disguise? *Fake* mustache maybe? Glasses – and a cap to hide my hair. That should do it."

Tom said nothing. Like the daffodils in the park the week before, he shook his head in worried *disbelief*.

---

disguise [dɪzˈgaɪz] clothing and other items which are used to hide a person's real identity
fake not real or genuine
disbelief [ˌdɪsbɪˈliːf] lack of ability to believe

Six

We spent the rest of the weekend trying to *persuade* Tom to join the team. Tom was totally alone apart from us. Both his parents were dead. He had come to the Hardy house last September, a year or so after Billy and me. It was his first foster. He was my age but wasn't in any of my classes at Moscrop *Secondary*. He was too clever.

On Sunday night I was in the boys' room. Billy and Tom were doing their homework. I was reading Jane Austen's 'Northanger Abbey'.

Billy put down his book. "I've picked our first bank."

"I friggin' told you," said Tom, "I'm not robbing any bank."

"You'd rather go to some unknown new foster?" I asked. "You've no idea how crazy these places can be."

"I know all about crazy," said Tom angrily. "I lived with crazy for a year. My dad."

Tom rarely talked about his life before the Hardys. We knew his mom had died of *cancer* and all he would say about his dad was that he 'went funny'.

"He *missed* Mom so much. He stopped going to his office

---

to persuade [pəˈsweɪd] to convince somebody to do what you want him or her to do

secondary [ˈsekəndri] *school* school that pupils go to at the age of 11 after primary school

cancer [ˈkænsə] very serious disease where the cells in one part of the body grow in a way that is not normal

to miss somebody *(here)* to wish that a person who is dead or has gone away could be with you again and worked in his garden instead. He was building a *shrine* to Mom. A real Japanese garden with trees, a *pond* and a *waterfall*. It was beautiful. But then he stole a garden *gnome* from the neighbors and put it in the center of the garden. A Japanese garden with a garden gnome!"

"You've got to be *joking*!" I said.

"But that wasn't the end. My dad brought home more gnomes and all kinds of garden things until the back garden was so full of *junk* that you couldn't see the beautiful Japanese garden – my mother's shrine. Then he began to fill the house with junk: kids' bikes, garden chairs and so on. The neighbors didn't care about the things he'd stolen from them. The poor man had just lost his wife and didn't know what he was doing. But finally one of them called the police. They came and looked and called Social Services. A mental health guy started visiting once a week. During one of these talks with the health guy, my dad had a *heart attack* and died."

shrine [ʃraɪn] place where a famous, holy or much-loved person is remembered

to joke [dʒəʊk] to say something funny to make other people laugh

junk [dʒʌŋk] old, unwanted things without use or value

heart attack [ə'tæk] serious medical condition when the heart stops working properly

I said, "It sounds as if your dad just wanted to be with your mom. He must've really loved her a lot."

"Yeah."

"I'm sorry you had to deal with that," said Billy.

"That's why we need to stay together," I said.

"That's why we have to raise the money," said Billy.

"I just don't think it'll work," Tom said. "You'll be *arrested* or even killed. Whoever heard of kids robbing a friggin' bank?"

"Just because we're kids doesn't mean we can't do it," Billy argued. "We've got a *foolproof* plan. We get the money, do a couple of handoffs and take the SkyTrain home. What could be simpler? If they catch us, we're too young to go to prison. Just a few days in *juvie*."

"What's juvie?"

"*Juvenile detention center*. Don't you know **anything**?"

Tom still wasn't convinced. He was starting to get angry. "Look, Billy. I like it here, but I don't want to spend the rest of my teens in a friggin' detention home."

"If we don't raise the ten grand soon," said Billy, "Janice and Joseph won't be an option."

"You've no idea what other fosters are like," I said, thinking of Mrs. Osberg.

Tom started doing his homework again, but he couldn't *concentrate*. After a while he turned to Billy. "You sure I wouldn't have to go inside the bank?"

---

to arrest [ə'rest] to catch a criminal and take him or her to the police station
foolproof ['fu:lpru:f] absolutely simple and safe
juvie ['dʒu:vi] = *Juvenile Detention* ['dʒu:vənaɪl‿dɪ'tenʃn] *Center* place where young criminals are kept (= detained)
to concentrate ['kɒnsəntreɪt] to think very carefully only about what you are doing

"I'm sure," said Billy with a big smile. "Just grab the bag from Nails and walk to the station. Simple? Yeah. The Three Musketeers. All for one and one for all."

Tom looked at me, then at Billy. "Okay, I'm in."

Tom was in. Yes!

"But we can't tell anyone, not even Lisa," I said.

"No," said Billy. "It's top secret."

"Now say after me," I *ordered*. "All for one and one for all."

We held up out hands, put them together, and cried, "All for one and one for all! All for one and one for all!"

That was how it started. It was history now, of course.

---

to order to tell somebody what he or she must do

Seven

April 4

So there we were after our first perfect bank robbery. Billy and Tom were sitting in the kitchen after bringing in the shopping and I was putting things into the *fridge.*

"Lisa's kitten is *cute,*" I said. "But is it a good idea for her. What if we have to move?"

Janice sighed. "We'll worry about that if it happens."

She looked so sad at the thought of losing her family that I almost told her about our plan to raise the money. Billy and Tom went out to see if there was any shopping left in the car and I went to fetch Lisa so we could set the table for supper. When I came back, Janice was looking thoughtfully out of the kitchen window. Billy and Tom were *chasing* each other round and round the car with the last two bags of shopping and laughing like crazy. Janice turned to me suddenly.

"The boys seem very active today, especially Billy. Has something special happened?"

I could feel my heart beating faster. "Like what?"

"I don't know. Billy seems to be on a high. He hasn't met a girl has he? Anything like that?"

---

fridge [frɪdʒ] kind of electrical cupboard where food can be kept cold
cute [kjuːt] *(especially AE)* very pretty or attractive
to chase to run after somebody and try to catch them

I laughed and hugged Janice. "Billy's fine. Don't worry about him. I'd know if there was anything wrong."

"Well, Nell, if you say so. You probably know him as well as anyone here."

* * *

It was Joseph's turn to *say grace*. "Thanks, Lord, for the family and the food. Amen."

"Amen," I said with the others.

I liked the way Joseph said grace. He really meant it. Not like some of the people in my other fosters who talked a lot about God and then turned around and...

Joseph and Janice always said what they meant and meant what they said. The Hardy home was the first place where I truly felt part of a real family. They weren't *rich*, but they gave us what we needed. We all ate the same food, no favorites. They were loving, and they treated us like we were special and important to them.

There wasn't much room for the six of us round the kitchen table. Tonight was spaghetti night, and I was getting tomato *sauce* on my *T-shirt*. *Lucky* it was a black T-shirt. Tom started telling me how to eat spaghetti.

"You turn it around your fork like this," he showed me. "You can use your spoon to help it you want."

---

to say grace to thank God for food
rich having a lot of money
sauce [sɔːs] thick liquid put on food to give it a special flavour
T-shirt [ˈtiːʃɜːt] shirt with short sleeves in the shape of the letter 'T'
lucky [ˈlʌki] having good fortune

Suddenly everybody was watching me. I could feel my face turning red, but Janice came to the *rescue*. "Nell is hungry, that's all. Eat up, Kiddo," she said, smiling.

But I had lost my *appetite*. I was practically a failure at school and now I couldn't even eat spaghetti properly.

I was angry at Mr.-Perfect-Tom-Okada. He's so smart and clever that he makes me sick.

As I *cleared* the table, I hoped Janice wouldn't *notice* that I'd eaten practically nothing.

* * *

Lisa took Pumpkin to bed with her.

I told her, "Pumpkin *sleeps* in his box on the floor."

"What if he gets *lonely* during the night?"

"He won't be lonely. We're right here if he needs us."

"Can I hold him while you read to me?"

"Yes, but afterwards he goes back into his own bed."

I often read to Lisa at bedtime. She is going into hospital to have her *tonsils* out in a month or so, and she's worried. She has never stayed in a hospital before. Lisa has been with the Hardys the longest of all of us, at least three years. Her parents died when she was four. Her first foster family made

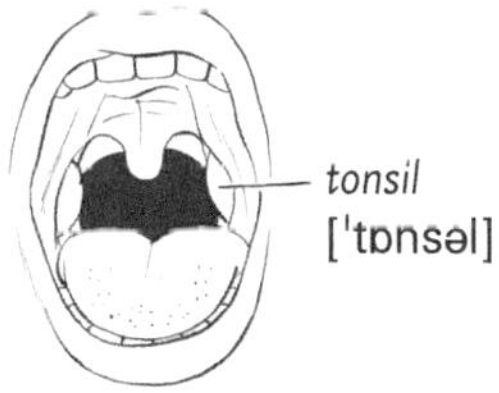

rescue ['reskju:] saving somebody from a dangerous or unpleasant situation
appetite ['æpɪtaɪt] feeling that you want to eat something
to clear to move things away from a surface
to notice ['nəʊtɪs] to see and remember something
to sleep – slept - slept to spend the night with your eyes closed
lonely ['ləʊnli] unhappy because you are alone

her sleep in a dark *scary basement* on her own. They also had a daughter who was *mean* to her. She came to the Hardys when her first foster mother got sick and had to give up fostering.

"Do you remember your mom and dad at all," I asked.

"Not much. Sometimes in the night I *wake* up and I can remember a nice warm feeling, like my mom is hugging me. Sometimes when I *smell* a certain kind of flower, I get the warm feeling, too. Maybe that's how she smelled. Real sweet, like that flower maybe?"

"What do you remember about your dad?"

"He used to let me *ride* on his shoulders, and it felt so safe up there with him holding my legs. I could see everything. I was the boss of the world, or the queen of England, or something..."

After I had finished reading the story, Lisa put the kitten into his box and *whispered* to me, "I don't ever want any of us to move from here."

"Don't worry, Sweetie," I told her. "None of us will ever have to move. Not if I can help it."

---

scary [ˈskeəri] making you feel afraid
basement [ˈbeɪsmənt] rooms of a house below the ground floor
mean [miːn] not very kind or fair
to wake – woke – woken to stop sleeping
to smell – smelt – smelt to use your nose to detect something
to ride – rode – ridden to sit on an animal, bike etc. and move from one place to another
to whisper [ˈwɪspə] to talk in a very quiet voice

Eight

April 5

The next day we were ready for our next success.

"Everything worked perfectly," said Billy. "And we took almost fifteen hundred bucks."

We were having a meeting in the boys' room. Billy was on his bed. Tom was sitting on the floor. He looked up. "That means we only need to do seven robberies."

"No problem," said Billy with a grin.

I stared at him. "That's a lot of robberies. I don't know if my heart can take it! Weren't you *scared*?"

He laughed. "Not a bit. I knew you two were *backing me up*. There was no *danger* to me. I enjoyed it."

"What about you, Tom?" I asked. "Were you scared?"

"Not really. By the time I got the bag it was almost all over. But I still don't like the idea of going to *jail*."

Billy looked at him. "We're only going to pick small banks and we're only taking small amounts of money. It's perfectly safe. Two handoffs. Two different bags. Foolproof. You did a great job, Tom."

He turned to me. "You did a fantastic job, too, Nails."

I was so pleased that I *blushed*.

---

scared [skeəd] very worried

to back somebody up to give somebody help

danger [ˈdeɪndʒə] very strong risk

jail [dʒeɪl] prison; place where criminals are kept for a long time and punished

to blush [blʌʃ] to become red in the face

* * *

I *tangled* with Tom that night. He'd said he never wanted to tangle with me, but it was his own *fault.*

It wasn't the boys' turn to use the bathroom first, but sometimes Tom *pretended* to forget. Once he had *locked* the bathroom door there was nothing Lisa and I could do but wait. And wait.

He said he didn't like going in after me because I left a mess, but my mess wasn't worse than anybody else's. The house's one-and-a-half bathrooms for six people was the problem.

Joseph and Janice had rules. Rule number one: maximum time in the bathroom at bedtime – ten minutes. Rule number two: everyone left the bathroom tidy for the next person. Rule number three: we took turns to go in first. Girls' night, boys' night.

When Tom came out we yelled at each other for a while. We tangled, but I was the first to *quit.* What was the use of tangling? Tom would never change. He wasn't *courteous,* like me. Or amiable. Sometimes he was quite *despicable.*

---

to tangle [ˈtæŋgl] to have a fight or an argument with somebody
fault [fɔːlt] *(here)* responsibility for a situation
to pretend [prɪˈtend] to behave as if something is true even though you know it is not
to lock to close a door with a key so that nobody can come in
to quit to stop doing something
courteous [ˈkɜːtiəs] *(old-fashioned)* polite
despicable [dɪˈspɪkəbl] *(old-fashioned)* very bad

Nine

April 6

Bank job number two was the Toronto Dominion Bank. There were only a few people in the bank – three customers and maybe four bank staff.

It was raining. I was standing outside the bank. I put my foot in the door as Billy walked up to the *counter* in his disguise. I could hear his scary voice. Then suddenly the young woman teller began to scream. "Help! Help!"

Everyone *froze*, including Billy.

Then he turned and ran. He dropped his disguise in my shopping bag. I didn't have time to think. I was so shocked I nearly fell to the ground. But I pulled myself together and walked slowly to the children's toyshop where Tom was waiting. He grabbed my bag, *stuffed* it into his backpack and walked off. I looked around. All was quiet. Nobody came *rushing* out of the bank.

I walked toward the train station, too scared to look over my shoulder.

* * *

Half an hour later we met in Billy and Tom's room.

Billy grinned. "Was that scary or what?"

---

counter ['kaʊntə] long desk or shelf between customers and staff in a shop, bank etc.
to freeze – froze – frozen *(here)* to stop moving or talking when you are suddenly at risk
to stuff [stʌf] to push something into a container with force
to rush [rʌʃ] to move very quickly

"That girl screaming scared me half to death," I said.

Tom cracked his knuckles and *glared* at Billy. "So your plan isn't exactly foolproof, Billy."

Billy shrugged. "We weren't caught, were we? There's not much I can do if the teller screams!"

"You looked and sounded too scary, Billy," I said. "It was like a *horror* movie. Just smile nicely and speak in a normal voice next time. Then the teller won't scream."

Billy laughed. "But I need to scare them a little. Maybe I should pull a crazy face or just cross my eyes!"

"It's not funny," said Tom. "We didn't make a cent."

Billy said nothing. But he looked relaxed, and I knew what he was thinking. Better luck next time.

Tom stared out of the window at the SkyTrain *tracks*. "My dad used to say '*Taste* everything but only *swallow* what tastes good'. It's an old Japanese *proverb*. What we're doing doesn't taste good to me."

I went to my own room. I was cold. I *crawled* into bed. And worried. What were we doing? I pulled the *blankets* over my head but I could still hear the *echo* of the bank teller's scream in my ears.

---

to glare to stare angrily
horror ['hɒrə] very strong feeling of shock
track railway line
to taste [teɪst] to put food or drink into your mouth to see what it is like
to swallow ['swɒləʊ] to move food or drink from your mouth into your body
proverb ['prɒvɜːb] wise old statement which gives good advice
to crawl [krɔːl] to move slowly, especially on your hands and knees
blanket ['blæŋkɪt] large, warm piece of cloth for sleeping under
echo ['ekəʊ] sound which comes back to what caused it after hitting an object far away

Ten

Tom had always *admired* and respected Billy.

When Tom started school, some of the other kids *bullied* him. Why? Perhaps because he was small, intelligent and Japanese Canadian. You can't get away from *racists* and you can't get away from bullies.

One day at school my best friend Liesel Fischer and I saw two tenth-*grade morons* Brad Stoker and Frank Drake bullying Tom at the far end of the sports field. We ran over to help but Drake and Stoker were too strong for us. Liesel and I grabbed Tom and the three of us ran back to the school building.

That night I told Billy what had happened.

"Leave it to me," he said quietly. "I'll see what I can do."

The next night Tom and I were washing up after supper. "Billy's a great guy," Tom began. "You should have seen how he treated those two morons who were bullying me yesterday."

"Drake and Stoker? What did he say to them?"

Tom grinned. "They were calling me names again – when Billy came up behind them and picked them both up by their jacket *collars* until they were dancing in the air

---

to admire [əd'maɪə] to like and respect a person for what he or she is or does
to bully ['bʊli] to hurt or say you will hurt somebody smaller or weaker than you
racist ['reɪsɪst] person who hates people of a different colour, nationality, race etc.
grade [greɪd] education level or school year number
moron ['mɔːrɒn] person with no intelligence
collar ['kɒlə] part of a shirt that goes round your neck

and could hardly *breathe*. Then he says real quiet 'I don't like to see you two bullying my *pal*'. Then he dropped them on the ground. When they're finally able to speak, Drake yells 'You gonna be sorry you did that'. Then Stoker says 'I'm telling the *principal* you nearly killed us'. But Billy stays calm and says 'Just leave my friend alone, or I'll pull your stupid heads off'."

"That's what he said? He'd pull their stupid…"

"That's exactly what he said, Nails."

"Wow. What did Drake and Stoker do?"

"Nothing. They were too scared. We just walked away and left them there. You should've been there, Nails. You'd have died laughing."

Brad Stoker and Frank Drake left Tom alone after that, which was one reason why we loved Billy so much.

And why Tom decided to take part in robbery number three.

---

to breathe [briːð] to take air into your body through your mouth or nose
pal good friend
principal ['prɪnsɪpəl] head of a school or college

ELEVEN

April 11

"We haven't hit a Royal yet, have we?" Tom asked Billy nervously. Crack-crack went his knuckles. We were sitting in a half-empty SkyTrain *carriage*, going from Burnaby to New Westminster.

It was only a week since our first holdup and now Billy had planned our third: the Royal Bank near the Columbia Street SkyTrain station.

Billy looked at Tom. "Stop playing with your *bones*! I wish you wouldn't crack your knuckles. It makes me think of what we've got inside us. Bones. Blood. *Yuck*!" He *paused* before answering Tom's question. "No Royal Bank yet. This is our first. We're being fair to everybody. We're giving all the banks an equal chance."

* * *

We followed our usual plan but I was worried. What if a teller screamed again and we had to run. I didn't think I could *handle* another scare like that.

It was raining as usual.

bone

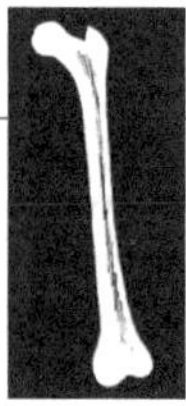

carriage ['kærɪdʒ] vehicle in which passengers travel on a railway or behind a horse

Yuck! [jʌk] you say this about something which you think is very unpleasant

to pause [pɔːz] to stop doing something for a short while

to handle ['hændl] to be able to deal with a situation or problem

Tom waited in a doorway about twenty steps away from the bank on the same side of the street.

Billy and I walked into the bank. It was a small, modern bank with no *security guards*. We had checked that a few days before. There was only one customer and three tellers, so two of them were available, a young man and a woman. I hoped Billy would choose the women. A woman might scream, but men played aggressive video games and could be dangerous. The woman had a friendly face.

I hated the moments before the robbery, but Billy loved them. He walked up to the young woman with the friendly face. I felt bad that we were going to scare her, but I told myself I was Nails – hard as nails – and we were doing this to keep the family together.

I opened the door for a woman with a small child and a baby in a *stroller*, and walked outside with my heart beating like the *engine* of a five-ton *truck*.

Seconds later the job was done. Billy was running toward the SkyTrain and I had the money and his disguise in my bag. He was clean.

As I moved away from the bank with my shopping bag, I wished I could feel as happy as Billy had looked. I pushed my bag into Tom's backpack. Now I was clean.

Tom walked slowly off toward the Columbia SkyTrain station.

---

security guard [sɪˈkjʊərəti‿ˌɡɑːd] person who protects a building or area from robbers etc.
stroller [ˈstrəʊlə] chair on wheels for pushing a young child along the street
engine [ˈendʒɪn] motor of a car, truck, ship etc.
truck [trʌk] heavy motor vehicle for carrying goods

I waited a few minutes, listening for the police *siren* before walking toward the station in the rain. I had a terrible *headache.*

* * *

When I got home I went straight upstairs to the boys' room. Billy was sitting on the bed eating an apple.

"Show us the money," he said, grinning.

Tom pulled the bag out of his backpack and emptied it onto Billy's bed. I counted the bills.

"How much?" asked Tom, cracking his knuckles.

"Four hundreds, eight fifties, fifteen twenties and two tens."

I tried to do the *math* in my head, but couldn't.

"Eleven hundred and twenty dollars," said *genius* Tom.

"Not bad," Billy said, eyes *shining*.

"Not bad," I said.

"Friggin' right!" Tom said. Crack-crack.

But we didn't *celebrate* this time. We just chanted "All for one and one for all".

"Great job, team," said Billy.

I went to my room, hid the money in the shoe box and wrote the amount on the lid.

Another victory for the Three Musketeers.

So why did I feel so bad about it?

---

siren ['saɪrən] equipment which makes a loud noise to warn you that a police car etc. is coming

headache ['hedeɪk] pain in the head

math *(AE)* mathematics; *(BE)* maths

genius ['dʒiːniəs] very clever person

to shine – shone [ʃɒn] *– shone* to give out or reflect light

to celebrate ['selɪbreɪt] to do something special to show happiness that something important has happened

TWELVE

April 12

The next day after school, Billy, Tom and I were *shooting hoops* in the park with Larry, a short grade-eight kid from school. Tom and me against Billy and Larry.

I had the ball, but Tom had other ideas.

"Pass! Pass it over here, Nails!" he yelled to me.

I threw it over Larry's head but it went wide of Tom.

Billy grabbed the ball and dropped it through the hoop.

"Ten!" Billy *shouted*, dancing around the court.

"If Nails would learn to pass...," *grumbled* Tom.

"You think you're so great? You *missed* more *shots* than you got in!" I yelled back at him.

"Well, at least I shoot sometimes!" he yelled at me.

"That's what I was trying to do when you yelled at me to pass!"

"Girls can't jump."

"Nor can you!"

I was tangling with Tom yet again. He was always telling me I couldn't do anything right. I couldn't play basketball. Couldn't even eat spaghetti right!

---

to shoot – shot – shot (here) to throw a basketball towards a *hoop*
hoop [huːp] circle of metal
to shout; to call something out in a loud voice
to grumble ['grʌmbl] to show your unhappiness when something has gone wrong
to miss (here) not to be able to achieve (or hit) something
shot the movement of shooting

Larry said he had to go. "Me too," I said. "See you guys later."

"Good game," said Larry with a smile.

"Yeah," I *muttered*. "Good game."

I said good-bye to Larry and walked home. The front door was not locked, and when I sat down on the stairs to take my running shoes off, I heard Janice and Joseph talking in the kitchen. I could hear that one of them was reading the newspaper.

"Look at this, Joe," Janice said. "There are lots of jobs for *full-time* workers in today's paper. I'm sure I'd make more money than working part-time at the school."

"Then you wouldn't be here for the kids," said Joseph. "They need you here when they get home from school."

"You're right," Janice said. "Of course, you're right. What about the bank. Any news on the *mortgage*?"

"They said they can't give us a second mortgage..."

"What about your brother Ron? He's got lots of money. I'm sure he'd help us out if you asked him."

"I called him last week. He's got no extra cash."

"Oh, Joe! What are we going to do?"

"I don't know, *Honey*. I just don't know."

They both sounded so sad that I wished I could just rush in and tell them that Billy and Tom and me would soon have the whole ten thousand.

---

to mutter ['mʌtə] to talk in a low, unclear voice

full-time lasting the whole of the working day

mortgage ['mɔːgɪdʒ] money which is lent by a bank on the security of a house or other property

Honey ['hʌni] form of address for somebody you love

Lisa's kitten came running out of the living room.

"Hey, Pumpkin," I whispered, but Janice heard me.

"Is that you, Nell?" She came out of the kitchen, smiling as usual. "You're back early."

"I *got tired* of shooting hoops," I told her. "I'm going up to my room to read for a while."

I carried the kitten up to my room. Lisa was at a friend's for the afternoon, so I had our bedroom to myself. I *lifted* the loose board and took out the shoe box with the money. There were three amounts on the lid.

Bank 1 – $1,450

Bank 2 – $0

Bank 3 – $1,120

That made a total of $2,570 so far. A long way to go.

I slowly counted the money, hoping it would be more, but it wasn't. It was too far away from the ten thousand dollars we needed. At this speed it would take a year before we had enough. And we only had a few months.

---

to get tired [ˈtaɪəd] *of* to have had enough of doing something
to lift to pull upwards

THIRTEEN

April 13

Billy chose the small Scotiabank in Surrey Place *Mall*, only a block from the SkyTrain station.

The mall was busy with shoppers. I was standing in the doorway of the Boston Pizza, *opposite* the bank.

Tom was waiting over at the ice-cream shop further along the mall. He'd be cracking his knuckles as usual. He never talked about being scared, but I knew he was.

Billy walked into the bank with his baseball cap pulled low over his eyes. Also as usual were his glasses, fake mustache, jeans, gray jacket.

I followed him into the bank. That wasn't the plan, but I couldn't stand not knowing what was going on. Tom wouldn't see us. His job was to wait. I saw Billy pass his note to the teller, an older woman, and I was close enough to hear him *growl*, "*Touch* the *alarm* and you're dead! Give me all your bills, and be quick!"

When I saw the *terrified* teller doing what Billy had asked, I left quickly and waited outside, holding my bag.

---

mall (AE [mɒːl]*)* shopping street, often with a roof, where no motor vehicles are allowed

opposite [ˈɒpezɪt] facing you on the other side of a street, room, table etc.

to growl [graʊl] to talk in a low, angry voice

to touch [tʌtʃ] to put your finger or part of your body on something

alarm [əˈlɑːm] piece of equipment which gives a warning that something is wrong

terrified [ˈterɪfaɪd] full of great fear

Billy came rushing out, dropped everything into my bag and *raced* off. A man came running out of the bank. He didn't notice me because of all the people walking by.

"Stop *thief*!" yelled the bank man.

Billy turned right into a shop. The man followed him.

Trouble.

I hurried over to the ice-cream shop and made my handoff to Tom. He stuffed my shopping bag into his backpack and *disappeared* among the shoppers.

The whole thing, from bank robbery to second handoff, had taken less than two minutes.

I hurried back to the shop to see if the bank man had caught Billy. He had. He was sitting on top of Billy, yelling like crazy. I felt *helpless*. What could I do? I had to stop myself from rushing over and pulling the bank man off Billy.

"He just ... robbed the bank!" cried the man, standing up. "Call the police!"

"Call the police," said the shop manager to his young *assistant*.

Billy stood up, confused. "I *gotta* go," he said.

"You'll stay here until the police arrive," said the bank man, putting two big hands onto Billy's arm. The manager took hold of Billy's other arm and they led him away to the office at the back of the *store*. I moved closer to see if I could help, but there was nothing I could do.

---

to race to run very quickly
thief [θiːf] person who steals something
to disappear [ˌdɪsəˈpɪə] to go away so that he, she or it cannot be seen
helpless not able to help
assistant [əˈsɪstənt] person who helps another person
I gotta (slang) I've got to
store shop

"Sit here," the manager said, pointing to a chair.

Billy sat down, looking *puzzled*, and waited.

The men waited.

I waited. My heart was thumping. My mouth was *dry*.

A police *officer* finally arrived. An experienced, older man, who began by questioning the bank guy. "How do you know this kid robbed your bank? Did you see him?"

"Yes, I did. Gloria – Miss Hampton – pressed the *silent* alarm. I saw him leave the bank and followed him in here. I didn't take my eyes off him for a minute."

"But this is just a big *dopey* kid," said the police officer. "Are you sure he's the person you saw?"

"I'm sure. He was wearing a disguise but I recognize his raincoat."

The police officer asked Billy how old he was.

"Fourteen."

The officer turned to the bank man. "Big for his age!"

Then he turned back to Billy. "This man says you robbed his bank. Did you?"

Billy looked shocked. "No, sir. This man *attacked* me. He's making a big mistake. He's hurt my back! Ow!"

"I'm going to *search* you," said the police officer. "Empty your pockets."

Billy emptied his pockets, groaning with pain.

---

puzzled [ˈpʌzəld] not able to understand and explain something
dry [draɪ] opposite of 'wet'
officer [ˈɒfɪsə] *(here)* policeman or policewoman
silent [ˈsaɪlənt] not making any sound
dopey [ˈdəʊpi] not looking very intelligent
to attack [əˈtæk] to use unexpected force against
to search [sɜːtʃ] *a person* to look at what a person has in his or her pockets or on his or her body

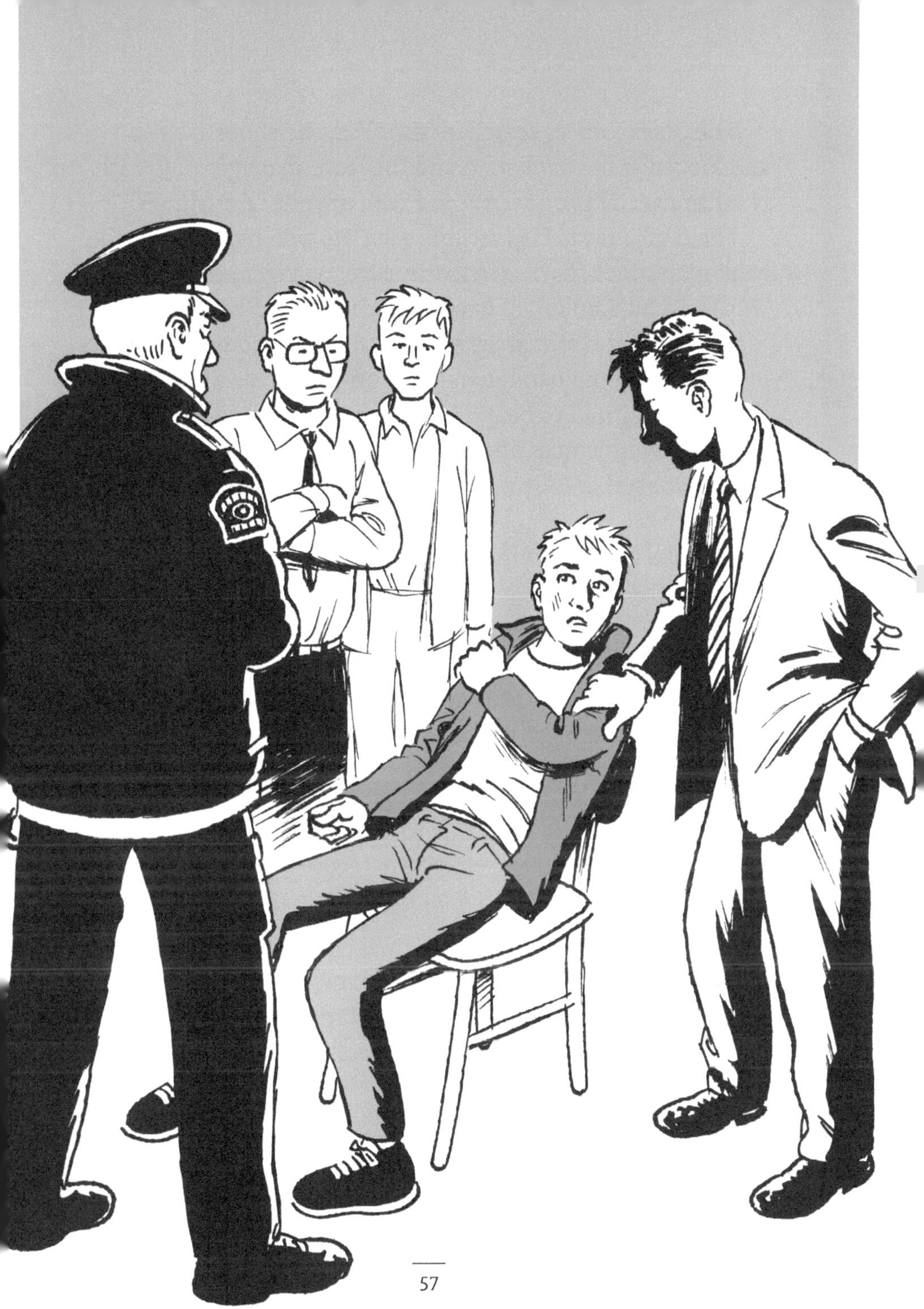

The police officer searched him. Then he shook his head and looked at the bank man and the store manager. "No cash. No disguise. Did you see the kid with anyone? A partner?"

I held my *breath*. Had anyone seen me with my bag? But the bank man shook his head and the store manager just shrugged. "My assistant Sam might have seen something," he said.

But when the officer asked him, all Sam said was that he had only seen the bank man jump on Billy. This was just what Billy wanted to hear. He turned to Sam.

"You saw this man attack me, right?"

Sam looked at Billy nervously. "I… I don't know…"

The police officer asked the bank man if he was sure the robber had come into the store. "Was he *out of sight* for even one second?"

"No," said the bank man. "I didn't take my eyes off him." But he didn't sound so sure and looked worried.

"Look, this kid here has got no money, no disguise. Could the real thief have got away?"

The bank man said, "But…"

I had seen and heard enough. Billy would be okay. He didn't need any help from me. I walked out of the store.

* * *

"They let me go," Billy told Tom and me later. "I gave them a *false* name and address. Then they let me go."

"I felt *awful* watching them question you," I said.

---

breath [breθ] the air which you breathe [bri:ð] into your body
out of sight [saɪt] a situation where something present cannot actually be seen
false [fɒls] not correct; fake
awful ['ɔ:fəl] very bad

"No more holdups," said Tom firmly. "That's it for me. You guys want to rob friggin' banks, you go right ahead, but I quit!" He cracked his knuckles. "You were almost caught. And if they get you then they get me too. I don't want to spend the rest of my life in prison."

"They don't send kids to prison," said Billy.

I said, "Stop it, you two. How much did we take?" I pulled my bag out of Tom's backpack, emptied it onto the bed and counted a hundred and fifty dollars.

"One-fifty," *moaned* Tom. "All that stress for a hundred and fifty friggin' bucks!"

We always expected thousands. In gangster movies, bank robbers were always counting big piles of hundred-dollar bills. For Tom Okada, a hundred and fifty dollars was a joke. I agreed with him but I didn't say anything.

"I quit," he said again. "The whole idea is stupid."

"It's not stupid!" I cried. "We're the Three Musketeers, remember?"

"The Three Musketeers is stupid and you're friggin' stupid too!" Tom left the room, slamming the door.

* * *

Later that night Tom and I were in the kitchen washing up. "Why do we do everything Billy says?" he asked angrily.

"Because it's the only way we can ever get our hands on that kind of money," I said.

"You look into his big blue eyes and listen to his voice

---

to moan to protest in an unhappy tone of voice

and you're lost," said Tom. "It's like *hypnosis*. But I can *resist* him. It's not a problem for me. But you're..."

I didn't listen to the rest. I finished the dishes and got out of the kitchen as quickly as I could.

* * *

Billy talked to Tom. *Charmed* him. We were walking to the bus stop on our way to school. Billy put one big arm round Tom's *thin* shoulder as if they were best pals.

"A hundred and fifty bucks isn't all that bad. It's more money than I ever saw before we started robbing banks."

"Billy's right, Tom," I said.

"I know it's a small amount," Billy went on, "but we'll get the ten grand in the end if we carry on."

"Sure we will," I said.

"But...," Tom began. But Billy cut him off.

"You're a good *buddy*, Tom. The kind of buddy I'd want on my side if things ever went wrong. You're like a brother. All I want is for us all to stay together at the Hardys'. We're a family – the only family any of us has."

Tom said, "I suppose so..."

"So it's worth fighting for. You can't let us down."

Tom agreed. The Three Musketeers were back together again.

---

hypnosis [hɪp'nəʊsɪs] a sleep-like state where a person's thoughts or actions can be controlled by somebody else
to resist [rɪ'zɪst] to stop yourself from doing something you really want to do
to charm to use kindness to make somebody do what you want
thin [θɪn] opposite of 'fat' or 'thick'
buddy ['bʌdi] very close friend

Fourteen

April 16

On Sunday the thin spring rain kept us in all day. Lisa had been busy all morning *painting* and playing with Pumpkin. But just as I was about to go to a meeting in the boys' room, she wanted to play Scrabble with me.

"Why are you always having meetings with the guys? What are these meetings about and why can't I come?"

"I'll try not to be too long. We'll play Scrabble later, okay?" I grabbed my math book.

The boys were waiting for me. After our last bank *disaster*, Billy had thought of a new method of *operation*. That was why we were having the meeting.

"Are we changing our method of operation because they caught you last time?" asked Tom.

"No. If you don't have any money on you when they catch you, there's nothing they can do. No, we need a change because a hundred and fifty bucks isn't enough. It would take us years to get the ten grand we need."

That's exactly what I'd been thinking.

"So what's the plan?" Tom asked.

"We hit harder. We rob **all** the tellers. Not just one."

"And how are we going to do **that**?" asked Tom.

"Simple. You're still our handoff man, Tom. But this time

---

to paint [peɪnt] *(here)* to make a coloured picture

disaster [dɪˈzɑːstə] very bad happening or something that is very disappointing

operation [ˌɒpəˈreɪʃən] *(here)* way of doing something

Nails and I go in together a few minutes before closing time. We're both in disguise. I order the tellers to put all their money on the counter. I pretend I've got a gun. Nell puts the money in her bag and we run for it. The cash and disguises go into Tom's backpack. We all *separate*. Then we all take the SkyTrain home as usual."

Silence. My heart went *numb*. I would have to go right in there and pick up the money.

"It won't work," Tom said after a while.

"Why not?" asked Billy calmly.

"It's too *risky*. More people in the bank will know what's happening. Until now only one teller knew about the robbery. And I don't like the idea of a gun."

"But there won't be a real gun. Just a pretend one."

"I don't even like the idea of a pretend gun."

Billy looked at me. "What do you think, Nails?"

It was hard to think with a numb heart. "It could work, I suppose," I said after a few seconds, surprised at myself. What was I saying? Was I getting used to the *excitement*? Was it because I'd do anything to keep us together? Or was I just trying to please Billy? I thought I knew the answer. I said quickly, "But I agree with Tom. It's too risky. What if someone in the bank has a real gun and starts shooting? If we're wearing disguises, they won't know we're just kids. Anyway, I couldn't pick up all that money. I'd have a heart attack."

---

to separate [ˈsepəreɪt] to go in different directions
numb [nʌm] unable to be felt; without physical feeling
risky [ˈrɪski] dangerous
excitement [ɪkˈsaɪtmənt] strong feeling that something happy, dramatic etc. is happening or going to happen

"Okay, forget it," said Billy, looking disappointed.

I hated letting him down. But it was Tom who spoke.

"I want to suggest a better handoff. I think I should be waiting round a corner, not on the same street as the bank. If someone sees the first handoff, they'll watch where Nails goes and see me. The idea of the second handoff is so that won't happen. If Nails walks round a corner, nobody watching her will see me."

"Good idea, Tom," said Billy. "Nails?"

"I like it, but it doesn't solve the problem of taking big risks for small amounts of money."

"We've made almost three thousand so far," said Tom. "That's almost a thousand dollars on each holdup."

I shook my head. "Don't forget the holdup where the teller screamed and we got a big fat zero."

"Okay, you're right, Nails. That makes about seven hundred for each holdup. I forgot we did four," said Tom.

"All the more reason to try out my new idea," argued Billy. "We should rob three or four tellers."

"Without me," said Tom.

"Me too," I said. "Too risky. I say let's continue as we are. No changes. Just Tom's idea, the changed handoff."

"Agreed," said Tom.

Billy shrugged. "Okay."

Fifteen

April 17

We chose our next bank by studying the phone book and a street *map*.

It would be a small Bank of Hong Kong in Vancouver's Eastside. Billy planned the holdup for ten to three o'clock on Thursday the twentieth. On Monday we left school early to check the bank out and decide where to do the handoffs. Tom around the corner and me right outside the bank *entrance*, as usual.

It was a nice little bank, and the SkyTrain station was only two blocks away.

"It's going to be a real *pleasure* to do this job," said Billy, who was getting more and more professional.

And more and more *charismatic*.

* * *

Billy and I walked into the bank about ten minutes before closing time. The bank seemed larger than it was because it was all glass and light. It was bright even on a rainy day like this one.

---

map drawing of the ground as seen from above to help people find their way
entrance ['entrəns] door or way into a building etc.
pleasure ['pleʒə] feeling or act of happiness
charismatic [ˌkærɪz'mætɪk] having a strong character that other people admire

Billy wore his usual disguise.

It was a cold day, but I was *sweating*.

There were two tellers with customers and an old guy looking through *brochures*. The manager's office door was closed, which was the way we liked it.

Billy walked up to the teller, who looked like a high-school kid not much older than me. Small, lots of make-up, *blond*. I left the bank and waited outside.

When Billy didn't come out after a couple of minutes, I knew something had gone wrong. I opened the bank door and looked inside. Billy was *wrestling* with the old guy who had been looking at brochures. He didn't seem so old now that he was holding Billy firmly by the arm.

Just as some of the other bank workers were coming to help, Billy pulled himself free and raced out of the bank. We ran down the street together. Billy stuffed his disguise and the *loot* into my bag and disappeared down a side street.

Trying to keep calm, I turned the corner and made my handoff to Tom, who calmly crossed the street and followed Billy to the station. I looked back up the street to the bank. Everything except my heart was quiet. Then I heard a police siren, and I hurried off to catch my train.

* * *

---

to sweat [swet] to lose water from your body during or after physical activity or mental excitement

brochure ['brəʊʃə] information booklet or magazine

blond with hair of a yellow colour

to wrestle ['resəl] to fight with a person by holding, pushing and pulling them

loot [lu:t] *(informal)* goods or money that has been stolen

I *collapsed* onto a chair. "That was close, Billy."

Tom threw himself onto his bed. "Too friggin' close! Who was the guy who jumped you? A security guard?"

Billy sighed and sat slowly down on his own bed. "I don't think so. Maybe he saw the teller crying, realized what was happening and jumped me."

"The teller was **crying**?" asked Tom in disbelief.

"I think that's what she was doing," said Billy quietly. "I saw *tears* but she didn't make any *noise.* Real quiet."

"Poor kid," I said, remembering my *impression* of her.

Tom said, "I don't like this. I never did. It's a *dirty* business. We're *messing* with people's lives."

I thought Tom was right. It was a dirty business. We were causing people pain.

"That bank had drop boxes. I saw them," said Billy.

This was new to me. "What's a drop box?"

"When the tellers have collected a lot of bills, they're supposed to drop most of them through a *slot* in the desk into a security box under the counter. They don't have a key to open this box, so most of the money is safe."

"Oh yeah," said Tom. "So what's this got to do with the girl crying?"

---

to collapse [kə'læps] to fall down suddenly and with force
tear [tiə] drop of water that comes out of your eyes when you cry
noise [nɔɪz] loud, often unpleasant sound
impression [ɪm'preʃən], feeling or picture you get of somebody or something from what you see of them
dirty ['dɜːti] *(here)* unfair and unpleasant
to mess with to have a negative effect on
slot narrow opening in a door, counter etc. through which letters, coins etc. are pushed

"Take a look in your backpack," said Billy *gloomily.*

We had completely forgotten about the money. Tom pulled out my shopping bag and emptied it on the bed.

Bills, bills and more bills – more than we'd ever seen.

Tom was speechless. I was *gobsmacked.*

I wondered why Billy was so gloomy after our most successful robbery. "You mean the girl had forgotten to put her extra bills into the drop box? That's why she was crying? She wasn't scared? She'll lose her job."

Billy looked even gloomier. "Yeah. Too bad for her..." He *brightened* a little. "But good for us."

We counted the money. But our hearts weren't in it.

The total was $2,750, the most we had ever taken.

We were more than halfway to our goal now, but we didn't celebrate. We were still thinking of the girl's tears.

"We should give it back," growled Tom, "and ask them not to fire the girl. Everybody makes mistakes."

Billy and I knew that giving the money back was not a practical solution, so we said nothing. And we were so much closer to our ten grand now.

"Surely there's something we can do," said Tom, walking nervously up and down the room. He was a pain sometimes when he grabbed the bathroom out of turn or *complained* about my ball-passing and my spaghetti-eating, but he had the softest heart of us all.

---

gloomy ['gluːmi] very sad and feeling that things will not get better
gobsmacked ['gɒbsmækt] *(informal)* completely surprised and shocked
to brighten ['braɪtn] to become lighter or happier
to complain [kəm'pleɪn] to protest that something is unfair or wrong and should be changed

Sixteen

April 21

The next day I was about to leave for school when Janice said she wanted to talk to me. She looked serious. I was worried. Had she found out something?

"It's Billy's birthday today," she began.

"Oh, I didn't know that."

"And I want to give him a little surprise tonight. His favorite supper, *lasagna*, and a big birthday cake."

I smiled. "He'll like that."

"I tried to tell Tom, but I couldn't get him alone before the guys left. Could you ask Tom to keep Billy busy for an hour or so after school – basketball in the park perhaps – so we'll have time to get supper ready."

"Sure. I could do that."

"But don't tell Billy. It's a surprise. And here's five dollars. Buy him a *giant bar* of Cadbury *Fruit* and *Nut* chocolate. That's his favorite. Now off you go!"

Everybody was in class when I arrived at school. Tom wasn't in any of my classes, so I'd have to talk to him at lunchtime. At lunchtime I found him in the *cafeteria.*

---

lasagna (BE lasagne) [lə'sænjə] Italian meal of minced meat between layers of flat pasta cheese and tomato sauce
giant ['dʒaɪənt] very large
bar unit in which chocolate, soap and gold are sold
fruit and nut ['fru:tənd,nʌt] type of chocolate containing nuts and raisins
cafeteria [,kæfɪ'tɪəriə] room in a school, factory etc. where people have lunch

"Got to talk to you," I said as I walked past his table.

He got up and followed me. "What's up?"

"It's Billy's birthday today, and Janice wants to give him a surprise supper. Can you keep him busy for about an hour after school while we get things ready?"

"Sure, no problem."

After school, the sun was shining as I walked toward the shops to get Billy's chocolate bar. Then I thought that perhaps I could get him something better – something from my favorite *second-hand* clothes store, Value Village. Billy was not much into clothes, but I went through the men's section until I found what I was looking for: a black *leather* jacket.

It was heavy – the real thing. I pulled it on over my raincoat. The leather was soft as butter and had a sweet leathery *smell*. It was far too big for me, but it would be fine for Billy. I smiled when I thought how *cool* he would look in it. He would look just like James Dean in the movies, and every time he put it on he would think, "Yes. I got this cool jacket from Nails."

But I got a shock when I saw the price: $17.00. Even with the $5.00 from Janice, all I had on me was $12.63.

I looked around. Nobody was watching. I could just walk out of the front door. I was a *big-time* bank robber. Stealing a jacket would be child's play. I looked at myself in a *mirror*.

---

second-hand already used by one person and now for sale to another
leather ['leðə] made out of the skin of an animal
smell impression of something which you get by putting your nose close to it and breathing in through your nose
cool (here) attractive in a way that makes people admire something
big-time very important or famous
mirror ['mɪrə] glass in which you look at yourself

My hair was almost as black as the jacket. "Yes," I *nodded* to my face in the mirror. "This jacket is perfect for Billy. I've got to have it." The Nails in the mirror nodded agreeably.

There was a sign beside the *cashier*: 'Value Village profits go to a good cause. Thank you.'

The cashier smiled at me, and before I could stop myself, I had asked her if she could keep the jacket for me while I went home to get more money.

"We keep things for just one hour," she said. "Okay?"

I knew where I could get the extra cash. I'd just take a few dollars from the shoe box. It was for a good cause, I told myself. A very good cause.

But once I was in the bedroom, I couldn't do it. That money was for a new bathroom so the four of us kids could stay here. Spending the money on other things would somehow make the bank robberies wrong.

Lisa came into the room.

"I'm making a birthday card for Billy," she said. "Would you like to sign it?"

"Sure." I looked for a pen. "Do you have any cash?"

"Not much. Maybe five or six dollars."

I told her about the jacket and that I needed just five dollars to buy it. "Then it could be from both of us."

"Fine," said Lisa. She gave me her money with a smile.

When I got back to Value Village there was a younger woman at the cash desk and no sign of the jacket. *Panic.*

"You were keeping a black leather jacket for me," I told the new cashier.

---

to nod to move your head up and down in order to say 'yes'
cashier [kæˈʃɪə] person in a shop or bank who handles money
panic [ˈpænɪk] sudden and very strong feeling of worry or nervousness

"We can only keep things for just one hour," she said.

Then I saw the jacket hanging on a *rack* waiting to go back to the shopping area. I grabbed it and paid for it.

When I got home, Janice called from the kitchen, "Nell? Is that you? Can you come and help me?"

"Did you get it?" asked Lisa, who was also helping.

"Yes," I smiled at her. "It's in this bag. He'll love it. Want to put your card inside?"

She did, and I put the bag on Billy's chair.

"That doesn't look like a chocolate bar," said Janice.

Before I could tell her, the guys rushed in. Janice pushed them out of the kitchen. "Can't come in yet," she told them. "We're not quite ready."

"What's going on?" Billy asked. "First I have to play basketball with Tom for an hour. Now we can't come into the kitchen! The food smells great and I'm *starving*!"

"Supper in twenty minutes," Janice said. "Upstairs! We'll call you down when we're ready."

Joseph came in as I was setting the table.

"We're ready now," Janice told him. "Call the boys."

"Surprise!" we yelled as the boys came in.

"Happy birthday, Billy," said Janice.

Billy's usually sleepy eyes opened wide in disbelief. "For me?" he said. "I didn't think you'd remember..."

"How could we forget one of our favorite kids in the whole world?" asked Janice, hugging him. "Happy fifteenth, dear."

Joseph shook his hand before hugging him. "Happy

---

rack long metal bar from which you can hang things
to starve to die of hunger

birthday, big guy." He *handed* him a small box. "This is from Janice and me."

Billy pulled opened the box. "Cool! A *digital* watch! Thanks a lot!"

"It's got an alarm," said Janice. "So no more *excuses* for being late or sleeping in."

Lisa pushed me forward. I got the bag from the chair. "This is from Lisa and me." I suddenly felt very *shy*. Would he like the jacket? Would he think it was *grungy*?

Billy pulled out the card first. "Who painted this?"

"I did, of course!" laughed Lisa in her excitement.

"Cool," said Billy, *kissing* her on the *cheek*.

Then he emptied the bag onto the chair and stood back in shock. "No way!" he breathed. "No fantastical way!" He pulled the jacket on and it fitted him perfectly. He put a hand into one of the pockets, shook his head, *stroked* the front and finally said in a quiet voice, "My dad had a jacket just like this. Same pockets – same smell. He was a big giant guy. Rode a *motorcycle*. He used to give me rides on it when I was real small. Haven't seen him since..." He stopped. Silence.

"Lasagna's ready, guys," said Janice. "Let's eat."

---

to hand to give using your hand
digital ['dɪdʒɪtəl] *(clock, watch etc.)* using numbers instead of hands to show time, speed etc.
excuse [ɪk'skjuːs] reason for not doing something
shy [ʃaɪ] nervous about what people think about you
grungy ['grʌndʒi] unpleasant, dirty or old
to kiss to touch with your lips
cheek side of your face
to stroke to move your hand slowly and lovingly across something or somebody
motorcycle ['məʊtəˌsaɪkəl] vehicle with two wheels and an engine

Billy nodded and looked at me. Could I see tears in his eyes? "Thanks, Nell," he said. "Thanks a lot." He turned to Lisa. "Thanks, *Princess*."

It was a lovely birthday supper.

Princess [prɪn'ses] daughter of a king and queen

Seventeen

April 25

Less than a week later, I was standing with Billy outside the Canadian Imperial Bank on Broadway. Tom was in position around the corner on Commercial Drive.

It was raining – as usual.

When we had checked out the bank a few days before, I had noticed that there was no place out of the rain, so I had brought an *umbrella*. Billy and I stood under it now.

Looking up, I saw the SkyTrain track over Ninth Avenue. Broadway Station was only *yards* away. I had my shopping bag under my left arm, open and ready.

Billy was waiting for a good time to go into the bank. The street was busy. A dirty *panhandler* was sitting on the step of a shop. An old woman asked Billy the way to the station, and he showed her. We waited a while longer.

"It's time," said Billy, and walked into the bank.

I waited outside, sweating as usual. Suddenly somebody grabbed my bag and pulled it from under my arm. It was the panhandler. He ran off with the bag. He must have thought there was money or something in it.

I wanted to shout 'Stop thief!'

---

umbrella [ʌm'brelə] →
yard [jɑːd] unit of measurement used in Britain and North America = 91.5 cm
panhandler ['pænhændlə] *(AE)* homeless person who asks other people for money

But then everybody would look at me, and this was the last thing we needed halfway through a bank robbery.

Now what? I had nothing for the handoff. I was still wondering when to do when Billy rushed out of the bank. I pulled my umbrella half closed and pointed it at the ground. Billy understood. He dropped everything into the umbrella and raced up the steps to the SkyTrain station. I hurried round the corner and emptied the umbrella into Tom's backpack. He disappeared.

I put the umbrella under my arm and was about to cross Commercial Drive when a hand on my shoulder pulled me back and my heart stopped.

"Hold it, kid. Show me that umbrella of yours." A man grabbed the umbrella, turned it over and shook it with one hand while holding me firmly with the other.

Was he from the bank? Had he seen Billy's handoff to me? My arm and shoulder were hurting. When he found nothing in the umbrella, the man looked surprised.

"Where's the money, you little thief?" he yelled into my ear. "What did you do with it?"

"No!" I yelled. I tried to pull myself away from him but I couldn't. "I'm not a thief! Not me!"

"*Liar*! I saw you! Outside the bank!"

"You're crazy! Let me go! You're hurting me. I don't know anything: Help! Help!" I yelled as loud as I could.

People were staring at us now. The bank man seemed less sure of his position. His hand was not holding my shoulder so firmly now. I pulled away and kicked him – first on one shin, then on the other.

"Aaargh!" he screamed in pain. I pushed him to the ground,

---

liar ['laɪə] person who does not tell the truth (= who *lies*) grabbed Janice's umbrella and ran across the street right in front of a bus, which nearly hit me. I rushed into the SkyTrain station, up the *escalator* and onto the *platform*. A train was just arriving. I got on and looked behind me. Nobody was following me. The train doors closed and I was safe. I collapsed onto a seat.

I had almost been caught, almost handed over to the police. I was terrified.

* * *

"What happened?"

Billy and Tom were waiting for me in their room.

"Have you been crying?" asked Tom, cracking his knuckles.

I was so *upset* that I wasn't able to sit down, so I walked up and down the room as I told my story.

"Were you really crying, Nails?" asked Billy.

"Crying? No way! But I was certainly scared."

"You had nothing on you but an umbrella," said Billy. "There was nothing to link you to the robbery."

"Except a *witness*," said Tom.

"He had no *proof*," said Billy. "What happened to your shopping bag anyway?" I told him.

"Just two bits of bad luck," said Tom. "How much?"

I counted it: $350. All that stress for $350! I threw it down onto the bed. Nobody said anything.

A SkyTrain *clattered* past below the window.

---

escalator ['eskəleɪtə] moving stairs
platform part of a station where you wait for a train
upset [ʌp'set] unhappy and worried because something unpleasant has happened
witness person who sees something happen
proof fact or facts which show that something is true
to clatter to make a loud metallic noise

Eighteen

April 28

A few days had gone by since our last holdup, and Billy had said nothing about our next one. It was as if he'd suddenly forgotten our mission. He acted strange for the rest of the week, hardly talking to anyone, coming home late from school every day. He went straight up to his room after dinner.

Janice knew something, but she wasn't telling.

* * *

"What's wrong with the big guy?" Tom asked me on the bus Friday morning. Billy was sitting up front on his own listening to music.

I shrugged. "I don't know. Maybe he's sick."

"I don't think he's sick. But he won't talk to me. You should talk to him, Nails. Maybe we can help him."

I didn't get a chance to talk to him that day, but the next day he was waiting for me after school.

"I need you to come somewhere with me, okay?"

"Okay." I said, following him. "Where are we going?"

"Hospital," he said simply, staring straight ahead.

"Why? You sick or something?"

"Course not. They said I could bring a friend."

"They? Who? Why are we going to a hospital, Billy?"

He looked down at me. "To see my dad," he said.

"Your dad? You've got a dad?"

Just a week ago Billy had said he hadn't seen his dad for a long time, so I thought he must be dead, like mine. His mom had disappeared a few years ago – visited a friend and never come back.

By now we had reached the SkyTrain station and Billy led the way to the platform for trains going west. A train arrived and we got on, but there were a lot of people on the train and it was only after Joyce Street Station that we could find a seat where we could sit together.

"Tell me about your dad."

He shook his head. "Later." He turned away from me.

We didn't get off the train at Broadway, so I knew we weren't going to Vancouver General Hospital. Burrard Street was the station for St. Paul's Hospital.

"Shouldn't we be getting off?" I asked Billy.

He shook his head.

We got off at Waterfront Station – the end of the line – and I followed Billy up the escalator and out onto Cordova Street. We walked through Gastown and along Water Street onto Powell. Where was Billy taking me? This was the part of town where the *drunks* and the drug *addicts* and the homeless people *hung out*. Well, we were criminals now. We belonged here.

* * *

We came to a small building with a sign on the grass in front of it: in big letters it said 'May's Place' and in small let-

---

drunk person who regularly drinks a lot of alcohol
addict ['ædɪkt] person who cannot live without alcohol, drugs, nicotine etc.
to hang out – hung – hung to spend time

ters 'The May Gutteridge Community Home'.

Billy led the way through the door to a small desk where an older woman in a *nurse's* uniform was sitting.

"Hello, Billy," she said. "Go right up."

I followed Billy up the stairs. This had to be the smallest hospital in the world. All the doors were open, and I counted six beds. Billy led me into a small room. The walls were painted light blue. The window looked out at another building. In the bed was an old guy with his eyes closed. He looked like he might be dead. Then I remembered why we were here. This was Billy's dad.

I sat down on a chair, wondering what I was doing here. I hated hospitals. The room was silent.

"Funny little hospital," I whispered.

"It isn't a hospital, it's a *hospice,*" he told me.

Then I remembered. A hospice is where people go to die.

Billy said, "He's got cancer real bad. The doctor told me that he can only live a few more days."

I had never been in a room with a dying person before. It was a bit scary. I looked at the *weak* old man's face. He looked nothing like Billy.

"Your dad lived around here?"

"Yeah. I only found out a couple of days ago. He's been here three weeks. Social Services called Janice."

On his birthday Billy had said that his dad had been a big guy. Maybe the man sleeping in the bed had been big once, but he wasn't big now. "Was that the last time you saw

---

nurse [nɜːs] person who looks after sick people
hospice ['hɒspɪs] place where sick people who are going to die are looked after
weak [wiːk] opposite of 'strong'

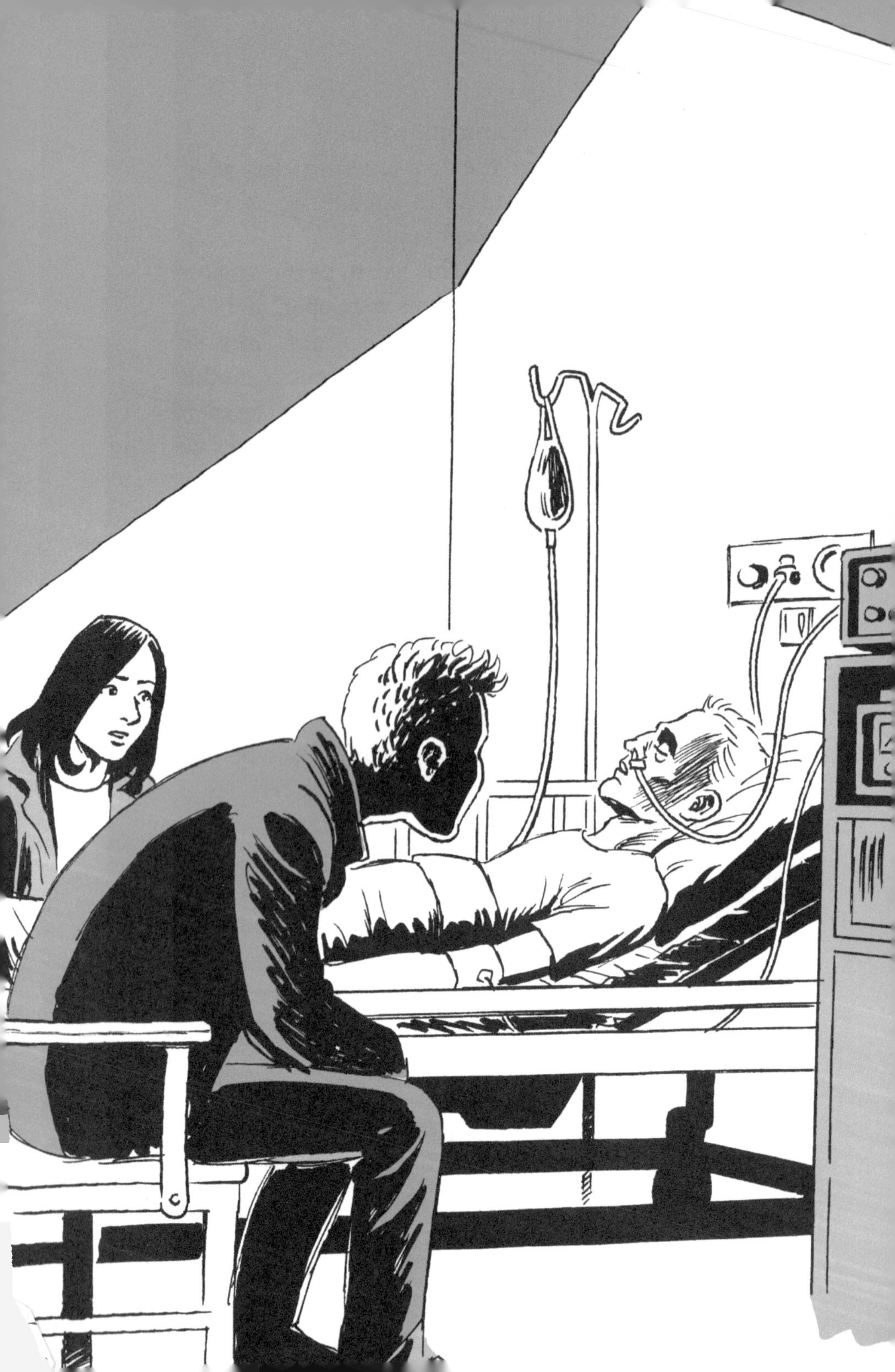

him, when you were small and he took you for rides on his motorcycle?"

Billy nodded. "One day he went off on his motorcycle and I never saw him again."

A nurse with short black hair came in, smiled at us, looked at the sleeping man, took his *pulse* and left. We sat in silence for a long time. Billy's dad didn't wake up.

Finally Billy sighed and said, "We'd better be going, Dad." His dad didn't move. You could only just see that he was breathing. We left.

Walking back to Waterfront Station, I said, "Why did you want me to come with you, Billy?"

"It helps," he said. "When he's *awake*, he never talks. He just looks at me. Or the wall. One day I was there he cried. I ask him things, but he never answers. I thought a pretty girl in the room might make him talk, you know."

I didn't say anything. I felt like crying.

* * *

We went again the next morning, not talking much during the forty-minute *trip*. Billy was very low.

The same nurse was at the desk. "Doctor Watterson just left, Billy. Your father is sleeping *comfortably*."

We sat down in his room to see if he would wake up. We didn't whisper this time. We talked in our normal voices.

---

pulse [pʌls] rhythm of the blood moving around your body
awake [ə'weɪk] not sleeping
trip short journey often made for pleasure
comfortable ['kʌmfətəbl] feeling physically relaxed or not under stress or in pain

I asked Billy if he knew anything about his dad's life before he came to May's Place.

"Dr. Watterson works for Mental Health Services. My dad's an *alcoholic*. But he had friends. He tried to help other people like himself. And Dr. Watterson tried to help Dad."

Suddenly I noticed that Billy's dad was awake. He stared at Billy with bright blue eyes. With those eyes, he suddenly looked very much like Billy.

"Hi, Dad," Billy said quietly.

His dad said nothing. But he began to stare at me.

"This is my friend Nails. She's in my foster. Her real name is Nell."

The old man tried hard to speak, and finally he managed to whisper, "Nell."

I smiled. "Hi."

His eyes turned to his son. "Billy," he whispered. He wanted to say more but couldn't. He closed his eyes, and although Billy talked to him, he was soon asleep again.

I asked Billy, "Was it *weird* seeing him here like this after all these years? Aren't you angry at him for leaving you?"

Billy's eyes *widened*. "Angry? I don't think so. I feel sorry for him, that's all, for *wasting* his life."

"What about what he did to **your** life?"

He shrugged. "I didn't have a dad when I needed one. Maybe I should be angry, but I'm not. He was weak. I won't ever be weak like him. I've promised myself that."

---

alcoholic [ˌælkəˈhɒlɪk] person who is an alcohol addict
weird [wɪəd] very strange
to widen [ˈwaɪdən] to make wider
to waste [weɪst] to use too much of something (to waste time) or not to use something properly

The nurse at the desk downstairs smiled as we left.

* * *

By now, Tom knew what was causing Billy's troubles.

"Want to come with us, Tom?" asked Billy on Sunday afternoon.

"Okay. If you're sure you want me to come."

This time the doctor and the nurse were in the room with Billy's dad. The doctor was a nice guy. "I've given him something to make him comfortable, Billy," he said.

We all went in and sat. The old man's eyes were closed. He was breathing with difficulty. He opened his eyes and looked first at Billy, then at me. He didn't seem to notice Tom. He slowly reached out a thin hand which Billy took in his big *fist*. He made a powerful effort to speak. "Billy – I'm ... so ... sorry ... Billy."

Billy put his arms around his father and hugged him. He spoke a few words into his dad's ear. I couldn't hear what he said because his dad was breathing so loud.

The old man's eyes closed, and in a second he was *asleep*. There was a smile on his thin *lips*.

Billy wanted to stay, so Tom and I went home mainly in silence. Tom stared out of the SkyTrain window, and when we got off at Patterson I could see from his eyes that he had been crying. He'd been thinking about Billy's dad or remembering his own dad – his lost family.

---

fist when you close your hand with your fingers inside, you make a *fist*
asleep [ə'sliːp] sleeping
lip top or bottom edge of the mouth

* * *

Billy stayed at the hospice all night and came home while we were eating breakfast. His face was white. He was tired.

Janice jumped up from the table. "How is he, Billy?"

Billy said nothing and looked at Janice helplessly.

We all knew.

Janice threw her arms around Billy. Joseph put his arms around Billy's and Janice's shoulders. Tom, Lisa and I joined them in a big family hug.

Nineteen

May 4

We left school early and took the SkyTrain to the city.

The Three Musketeers,

I had a bad feeling about this holdup.

It was raining and there was a cold wind. I had the first signs of *flu*: a headache, and my nose was running.

Billy and I took up our positions outside the Vancity Savings Bank. Tom was out of sight around the corner.

This was our seventh bank robbery. Wasn't seven supposed to be a lucky number?

I could see that the bank was busy. Maybe Billy's planning wasn't as good as he thought. A guy in a Honda across the street was drinking coffee from a plastic cup and watching people. He looked across at Billy. Was he a *detective*? Had the police finally caught up with us?

The man stared at me. Maybe he wasn't a *cop*. Maybe he was hoping to pick up a street kid, offering money for sex. I turned my back on the guy.

I checked my watch. It was 1:22 PM.

Billy was still outside the bank. What was happening?

The guy in the Honda drove away, and I felt better.

---

flu [fluː] short for 'influenza', a common illness involving a high temperature a feeling of weakness and a running nose
detective [dɪˈtektɪv] person who tries to stop or solve crimes
cop *(slang)* policeman

Finally, at 1:26 PM, Billy gave the signal and walked into the bank. I crossed the street and waited outside.

Billy came flying out, dropped his cap, mustache, glasses and the loot into my bag and rushed round the corner. I moved down the street in the other direction, turned the corner and made the handoff to Tom. Tom grabbed my bag and disappeared. It was 1:32 PM.

I walked back toward the bank, trying to keep calm.

The Honda was back outside the bank. The driver was watching me. Was I going to be arrested? Thank God I didn't have the money. Had the guy seen the handoffs?

"Hey! Girl!" he called as I walked past. I turned to face him. He certainly looked like a cop until he started talking to me. He was old and *ugly*, with yellow teeth and wet lips. "You're real pretty," he said. "You know that, girl? You want to make fifty bucks?"

I turned away and ran all the way to the station.

When the train arrived I got on and collapsed into the nearest seat. My nose was *dripping* and I had run out of *tissues*. I was wet. I was cold. My headache was worse.

Tom pushed his way in just as the doors were closing.

"What are you doing here?" I *hissed*. "You're supposed to take a different train home."

"Quit telling me what to do," he hissed back. He took my shopping bag out of his backpack and sat down.

I grabbed the bag. "Look. Billy said the only way this will work is if we all do what we're supposed to do."

---

ugly [ˈʌgli] opposite of 'pretty'
to drip to fall in small drops or to allow small drops to fall off something
tissue [ˈtɪʃuː] piece of soft paper into which you blow your nose
to hiss to make a sound like water falling on a very hot surface

"I'm sick of it," he muttered. "I'm sick of you. And I'm sick of Billy."

"We'll get caught if we're not careful."

An old woman turned and stared at us. Had she heard? I stared angrily back at her. She turned away quickly.

"Anyway," I went on. "You shouldn't be here."

"Look," he said. "Why should I stand out there in the cold waiting for the next train just because you say so?"

"It's all part of the plan. Surely you understand that?"

"I'm sick of the whole thing. It's just not worth it."

"How can you say that? If we don't stay together they will probably send you to live with someone like old Mrs. Osberg."

Tom shook his head. "Look," he said quietly. "What we're doing is wrong. Just wrong. And it isn't working. We'll never get ten grand." He cracked his knuckles. "I've had enough. I won't let Billy persuade me again. You guys won't be able to boss me around any more."

He had quit for good this time. I could tell.

When we got to Patterson Station, I tried to get away from Tom so that nobody would see us together. But Tom stayed right behind me until we got home, and when we got to the front door we were both out of breath. He took out his door key before I had time to take out mine. He opened the front door and pushed into the house ahead of me.

He stopped dead. I ran into him.

Uh-oh. Janice was there. She wasn't supposed to be home until four.

"Hi there, you two. You're early," said Janice, who was just coming out of the kitchen. "Want a cup of tea? I've just made some."

"Tea sounds good. Thanks," I said. Then I realized that I was still holding the bag with the money.

Janice looked at me closely. "You look awful, Nell." She touched my *forehead*. "And you're hot. You need a nice warm cup of tea and an aspirin. Then a nice hot *shower*."

I followed her back into the kitchen. Tom was right behind me. Janice gave us a cup of hot tea each.

"Did they let you out of school early today?"

I had to think quickly. "The teachers let us go home early because they have this very important meeting..."

"That's a lie," hissed Tom, cracking his knuckles. "We *skipped out*. We've been skipping out of school all this month."

Janice said with a laugh, "Skipping out of school? I don't get it." But her laugh sounded somehow *uncertain*. "You're good kids. Good kids don't skip out of school."

"Us? Good kids? Ha!" Tom laughed *bitterly*. "That's a joke! You know what your good kids have been doing?" He turned his back on me. "We've been robbing banks."

---

forehead [ˈfɒrɪd / ˈfɔːhed] the front of your head above your eyes
shower [ˈʃaʊə] piece of equipment that you stand under to wash your whole body
to skip out of school to leave school early without permission
uncertain [ʌnˈsɜːtn] not sure
bitter opposite of 'sweet'

I was *horrified*. Tom had promised to keep our secret.

Janice was so shocked that she couldn't speak. Finally she said, "Robbing... I don't understand."

"Show her the money, Nails," Tom *demanded*.

I was still holding the shopping bag. I stood up.

"Come on," growled Tom. "Show Janice what's in your bag. Show her what her good kids have done!"

I *backed* away, holding the bag close to my *chest*.

But Tom pulled the bag out of my arms and emptied it onto the kitchen table. Billy's fake mustache, glasses and cap fell out. A few bills *fluttered* out of the cap.

Janice picked up the bills. "You want to tell me where this money came from?" she asked me quietly.

I shrugged.

"From a bank in Vancouver," Tom told her. "We didn't get much this time, though."

"This time?" Janice asked, her voice cracking. "You mean..."

We heard the front door open. Billy came in, grinning widely as usual. But his grin *vanished* when he saw his disguise on the table and the money in Janice's hand.

"Billy is in on this, too," Tom told Janice. "We're bank robbers, all three of us."

Janice dropped the bills as if they were suddenly red hot. "I don't believe it," she whispered.

---

horrified [ˈhɒrɪfaɪd] filled with horror
to demand [dɪˈmɑːnd] to tell or order a person to do something
to back away to move backwards
chest front part of the body
to flutter [ˈflʌtə] *(here)* to fall slowly while moving from side to side
to vanish [ˈvænɪʃ] to disappear

"It's true," said Tom.

Janice stared at us with huge eyes. Then she tried to pull herself together. "Come and sit down all of you."

We sat. Billy stared at Tom, wondering what was happening. Tom wouldn't look at either of us. I hated him. He had *betrayed* us. He was our personal Judas.

Janice picked up the phone.

Billy *patted* me on the shoulder. "Don't worry."

How could I **not** worry when my life was collapsing?

Janice was phoning Joseph to ask him to come home.

While we were waiting for him, Janice started asking questions. "Where is the rest of the money?"

I told her. She told me to go and get it. I went upstairs and brought the shoe box down. The total on the lid was a *measly* $5,470. We were only halfway to our goal. I put the box on the kitchen table and Janice looked inside, *gasped* and put the lid back on as if it were full of deadly *tarantulas*.

By the time Joseph got home, Janice knew most of what had happened. She explained it to him. He looked at us in turn. His kind face looked disappointed and sad.

"Just how many banks did you rob?"

"Six," I said.

"Seven," said Billy, "if you include one failure."

Joseph's eyes widened. "Seven! How could three kids rob seven banks and not get caught? I don't believe it!"

Tom told all. Janice was trying hard not to cry. They lis-

---

to betray [bɪˈtreɪ] to give away a secret in order to harm somebody
to pat to touch softly with your hand several times in a friendly or comforting way
measly [ˈmiːzli] *(informal)* very small and disappointing in size
to gasp [gɑːsp] to breathe in with surprise
tarantula [təˈræntjʊlə] large spider with a poisonous bite

tened without interrupting. When Tom had finished, Joseph asked, "But why? Why do such a crazy thing?"

I said, "Because we don't want to leave here. We don't ever want to leave you and Janice. The money was for a new bathroom. We had no other choice!"

Janice *murmured faintly*, "New bathroom?"

By now, with my headache and running nose, and the bad way I was feeling about *disappointing* Janice and Joseph, I could no longer hold back the tears.

"That's why we needed ten grand," I cried, "and we would never have got caught if Tom hadn't told you. We needed it for a new bathroom so we could stay together."

Joseph shook his head. His voice got louder. "Do you kids realize how dangerous it is to rob a bank? You could be shot by security," he said, walking up and down the kitchen to control his *anger*. "You could be killed! And other people in the bank could be killed! For what? For a few *lousy* dollars! Were you on drugs?" He looked at me.

"We don't do drugs," said Billy. "You know that."

"I don't know anything after this," said Joseph.

Janice said, "Take it easy, Joe."

Finally he *cooled down*, stopped walking up and down the room and looked grimly at each of us in turn.

"You know what we've got to do, don't you?"

---

to murmur ['mɜːmə] to talk in a very quiet voice
faint very difficult to hear, see, feel etc.
to disappoint [ˌdɪsə'pɔɪnt] to make somebody feel unhappy because something or someone's behaviour is not as good as expected
anger ['æŋgə] strong feeling of wanting to hurt or criticize somebody who has hurt you
lousy ['laʊzi] unimportant or of very low quality
to cool down to stop being angry

"What?" I said through my tears.

"Call the police, of course," said Joseph.

Tom looked up. "Why can't you just *punish* us? We're only kids. We can't go to jail," he said.

"We've got no choice. Robbery is a crime, and crimes must be reported to the police. What did you think would happen?" Joseph asked him, *amazed*.

"I thought you'd take the money and get the friggin' bathroom," said Tom, almost angrily.

"We couldn't do that. It's stolen money. We could never use stolen money. Don't you see that? You kids haven't thought this through very well, have you?"

He sighed deeply as he reached for the phone.

"Wait," I said. "We must go to the police ourselves. It would keep you and Janice out of it. It's not your fault."

"We don't want to be kept out of it," said Janice. "It **is** our fault. We knew something was going on. We should have asked more questions. I blame myself."

"I'm not *turning myself in*," Tom said. "No way!"

Janice got up to make more tea. We watched her in silence. "Turn yourselves in or..." We waited.

"... or we call the police," Joseph finished. "Now."

I said, "Don't worry, Janice. We'll do it."

Joseph said, "I'll drive you there."

I looked at Billy. Billy put a hand on Tom's shoulder. Tom took a deep breath. "Okay," he said. "Let's do it."

"Trust us," I said to Joseph. "We'll SkyTrain over."

---

to punish ['pʌnɪʃ] to make somebody suffer because he or she had done something wrong

amazed [ə'meɪzd] extremely surprised

to turn oneself in to go to the police and tell them that you have broken the law

I felt better after I had taken a hot shower and put on some dry clothes. I put the money into my shopping bag and we SkyTrained to the police station.

We were the Three Musketeers, still together even if our secret was out. Even though Tom had betrayed us.

It was strange. I was feeling *relieved*, almost happy, and so was Tom. I could see it in his face, and he hadn't cracked his knuckles since he had told Janice what we had done.

I wasn't sure about Billy. Perhaps he was looking forward to our new *adventure* with the police. Anyway, the Three Musketeers would face the *challenge* together.

I'd never been in a police station before. I looked across at Billy's calm face and wondered if he had.

Two police officers in blue shirts were sitting at a high counter talking to people. Two more officers sat at a table behind them. One was telephoning, the other was writing. We sat on a *bench* at the back of the room and waited. When there was nobody else at the desk, one of the officers, an older man with thin, gray hair saw us.

"You waiting to see somebody?"

I *stepped* forward. Billy and Tom followed. The counter

---

relieved [rɪˈliːvd] happy that something bad or unpleasant is over
adventure [ədˈventʃə] very exciting, dangerous or interesting experience, journey etc.
challenge [ˈtʃælɪndʒ] job or task that is very difficult to do
bench see illustration on page 94
to step to put one foot in front of the other when walking

corridor ['kɒrɪdɔː]
bench

was as high as my nose. "We've come to *confess*," I told him.

Billy nodded. "We're turning ourselves in."

Tom cracked his knuckles.

The officer smiled, "Yeah? Robbed a bank have we?"

"Six," I said.

"Seven," said Billy.

The officer turned to his partner, laughing. "You hear that, Beckett? These kids have been robbing banks. She robbed six and he robbed seven."

"Thirteen!" his partner cried.

"No," said Tom, "seven in total."

"Oh, well now, seven's not so bad." He laughed.

I held up the bag. "And we're returning the money."

The officer named Beckett looked in the bag, and his eyes nearly dropped out of his head. "Well, I'll be..."

The first officer looked into the bag and his grin disappeared. "How much money is in here?" he asked.

I shrugged. The total wasn't important any more. Why didn't they just arrest us and lock us up?

"Stay right there," Beckett told us. He picked up a phone and spoke into it. Then he hung up and stared at us, shaking his head. "Come with me."

We followed him down a *corridor* to a door marked *Chief Inspector* Teal. Beckett *knocked* at the door and pushed us into the office. Chief Inspector Teal was wearing a *suit* and a green *tie*. "Sit down," he said as he took the bag of money

---

to confess [kən'fes] to say that you have done something bad like a crime
chief inspector ['tʃiːf‿ɪn'spektə] fairly important police officer
to knock [nɒk] *(here)* to hit a door with your knuckles
suit [suːt] trousers and jacket of the same colour or pattern that are worn together
tie [taɪ] narrow piece of cloth that is tied around the collar of a shirt

from Officer Beckett. But Beckett had to fetch another chair before we could all sit down.

Billy sat on one side of me, Tom on the other.

Officer Beckett left again. The Chief Inspector began.

"Now what's all this about? You robbed some banks, is that right?" He spoke in the friendly voice that adults often use for children. He smiled at us in a way that a father smiles at his clever but *naughty kiddies*.

I pointed to the bag on his desk. "The money we stole is there, every penny."

The Chief Inspector emptied the bag onto his desk. The bills fell out and formed a paper *mountain* in the middle of the desk. A few of them fluttered to the floor.

He stared at us, then at the money, then at us again. He picked up the phone. "Beckett? Bring in our latest files on bank robberies, will you?"

* * *

Chief Inspector Teal and another detective named *Sergeant* Finch asked a hundred questions and recorded our answers on *tape*. I thought the questions would never end, but finally they took us home in a police car. Then they talked to Janice and Joseph for about two hours.

Ten days later we received a *summons* to appear at the juvenile court the following week.

tape

naughty [ˈnɔːti] behaving badly
kiddie [ˈkɪdi] *(informal)* young child
mountain [ˈmaʊntɪn] hill that (in Britain) is over 1,000 feet high
sergeant [ˈsɑːdʒənt] police officer on the second level (after 'constable' and before 'inspector')
summons [ˈsʌmənz] official order to come to a court hearing

Twenty-two

May 22

The judge was a woman with a long thin nose. She listened to an *energetic* young *lawyer* in a gray suit and red tie, who described the crimes. She watched the security videos, but the person leaving the bank in each case could have been anybody. It didn't look like Billy.

Then the judge listened to our *defense* lawyer, Miss Farthingale, who looked only a couple of years older than me. She had blond hair and wore a black suit. She had come to the house a few days ago, with more questions.

Miss Farthingale told the judge about the bathroom problem. "They were trying to raise money to have an extra bathroom *installed* so they wouldn't have to leave their foster home, *Your Honor*. They did not want to see their family broken up. They were prepared to risk anything to stay together. But they did not use *weapons* during the robberies and are very sorry for what they have done. The children turned themselves in and returned all the stolen money. Not one penny is *missing*. They

---

energetic [ˌenəˈdʒetɪk] very active; full of energy
lawyer [ˈlɔɪə] person who works in a law office
defense (BE defence) [dɪˈfens] *lawyer* lawyer who speaks in court for people who are supposed to have done something bad
to install [ɪnˈstɑːl] to set up one or more pieces of new equipment
Your Honor (BE Honour) [ˈɒnə] respectful way of addressing a judge
weapon [ˈwepən] instrument for hurting or killing somebody
to be missing not in its proper place

saw their cause as a *noble* one, Your Honor."

"They saw robbing banks as a **noble cause**?" said the judge, her eyes opening wide.

"Yes, Your Honor," said Miss Farthingale firmly. "They wanted to stay together in the family that provides them with love and security. If the British Columbian Social Services had done their job properly, there would have been no need for these robberies in the first place."

"They could have been killed or seriously hurt if a security guard or a police officer had started shooting. Robbing banks is a dangerous game, noble or not." She glared down at us from her *throne*.

I glared back.

Billy looked as if he was enjoying himself. He was smiling. Tom was cracking his knuckles again.

The judge *adjourned* the case for a week.

* * *

A week later we were back in court with Joseph and Janice. We sat at a table and waited for the judge to announce her decision.

"First of all," she said, "I want to *commend* the three of you for what you tried to do for your foster parents. I fully understand that you wanted to help them. You did not want to be taken away from the home and the people you love. What I do not understand is why the Hardys' home, which

---

noble ['nəʊbəl] good and able to be admired

throne [θrəʊn] official seat of a king or queen

to adjourn [ə'dʒɜːn] to stop a meeting, court hearing etc. and say that it will start again on a future date

to commend [kə'mend] to say publicly that somebody has done a good or noble thing has helped many young people, does not get more help from Social Services. We have looked into the matter, and I can tell you now that money has been found to build the extra bathroom within the next few months."

I grinned at her. "Your Honor, does that mean that we won't have to move?"

"Ssshh," whispered Miss Farthingale.

But the judge answered my question. "Yes, young lady. That's exactly what it means."

I turned to my musketeers and we smiled at each other. I felt like yelling 'Three *cheers* for Her Honor!' but managed to sit still and quiet while the judge went on.

"Bank robbery is a serious crime. The three of you confessed to seven robberies. You have returned the money but you put the lives of *innocent* people in danger. So you must be punished and made to understand that breaking the law has serious consequences. Nell Ford, Billy Galloway and Tom Okada, please stand."

We stood, shoulder to shoulder, like the Three Musketeers. What would our *punishment* be?

The judge took a deep breath. "I must deal with you firmly. I *sentence* each of you to twenty-eight days in the Vancouver Juvenile Detention Home, starting at the end of the school year, on July third. After that, you will do three hundred hours of community service. Ten hours a week for seven months. One month for each bank."

---

cheer [tʃɪə] loud shout which expresses great happiness
innocent [ˈɪnəsənt] having done nothing bad or wrong
punishment [ˈpʌnɪʃmənt] action of punishing somebody
to sentence [ˈsentəns] when a judge tells a criminal what his punishment will be, he or she *sentences* that person

* * *

When we got outside with Joseph and Janice, I didn't know whether to feel *depressed* or *excited*. "You'll get enough for the extra bathroom and we can stay together."

"I can't tell you," Joseph began, "how happy..."

"...it makes us," Janice finished.

"Great!" cried Billy, grinning like an *idiot*.

"Friggin' fantastic," Tom agreed.

Joseph said, "You won't think a month in juvie is so fantastic, or..."

"...the three hundred hours of community service," finished Janice. "It's going to be hard work."

"A whole month of juvie!" I moaned.

"Probably the hardest month of your life," Joseph sighed. "You have to work from early morning to night – I've seen it, so I know. Kitchen work, field work..."

We groaned.

"Don't complain," said Miss Farthingale. "It's a very light sentence. The judge was easy on you."

"Easy!" said Billy. "What does she do for hard?"

"I knew we'd end up in friggin' jail," moaned Tom.

"Plus three hundred hours community work," groaned Billy.

I said nothing. What could I say? I was so happy not to be leaving Janice and Joseph that I didn't care about the sentence. I would *survive*.

---

depressed [dɪ'prest] sad and full of negative thoughts
excited [ɪk'saɪtɪd] happy that something good is happening or will happen
idiot ['ɪdiət] stupid person
to survive [sə'vaɪv] to go through a difficult time and come out alive

Twenty-three

July

Before I knew it, school was out for the summer and I had to say good-bye to Liesel. I didn't tell her I would be spending most of July in juvie. She would want to know why, and I wasn't going to tell her – or anybody – our *incredible* story. They would think we were making it up.

I told my mom that I was going away on a trip.

"A month soon passes, especially if you're busy," said Joseph. "You're all strong. You'll be fine."

Janice tried to smile. "We'll be back for you on the thirtieth. The house will be so empty without you."

"You both *deserve* a break from us all," said Tom.

I was separated from the boys and felt totally alone. Tom and Billy were lucky. At least they had each other.

The less said about juvie, the better. Breakfast, as much as you wanted, was at six. If you were late, you got nothing. There were eight girls from eleven to sixteen years old, and Joseph was right about the work. It was hard. We started at seven. The *supervisors* were *strict* but fair. I worked mostly in the kitchen and the *laundry*. Work ended at six. Then it was

---

incredible [ɪnˈkredɪbl] difficult or impossible to believe
to deserve [dɪˈzɜːv] to have earned the right to something
supervisor [ˈsuːpəvaɪzə] person who makes sure that people work or behave properly
strict expecting people to keep to the rules and do what you say
laundry [ˈlɔːndri] building or room where clothes are washed, ironed etc.

supper and back to a *dormitory* of twenty beds. Lights out was eight o'clock.

For the first week I *ached* all over.

Most of the other girls had been in juvie before. They bullied me because it was my first time. I had a fight after lights out with an older girl. I hit her in the *stomach* and kicked both her shins. The other girls screamed with excitement. The night supervisor, a big woman called Miss Coke, stopped the fight and woke the two of us up at four-thirty the next morning to run around outside in the cold for thirty minutes wearing only our *pajamas*.

Seeing Janice and Joseph when it was all over was like having Christmas and *Easter* and my birthday and my mom's birthday all at the same time.

Tom had a black eye and a cut on his forehead, but he was grinning like a boxing world champion.

Billy looked as if he had enjoyed being in jail. He was an inch taller and looked like an *explorer* just back from the *jungles* of darkest Africa.

---

dormitory ['dɔːmɪtri] room where a group of people all sleep
to ache [eɪk] to feel pain
stomach ['stʌmək] organ of the body where food goes first
pajamas (BE pyjamas) [pe'dʒɑːməz] clothes which you wear in bed
Easter ['iːstə] time of year when Christians celebrate Christ's death and rebirth
explorer [ɪk'splɔːrə] person who finds out about unknown parts of the world etc.
jungle ['dʒʌŋəl] thick forest in a hot, wet country

Twenty-Four

Saturday night, a week later, I was sitting on my bed trying to brush the juvie out of my hair and mind.

"Will you brush my hair when you're finished?" Lisa asked. She was sitting on her bed with Pumpkin. She would be going to hospital for her *operation* on Monday.

"Of course, I'd love to brush your hair. Want me to *braid* it? It would look so cool with lots of little braids."

"Sure," she said, stroking Pumpkin. But she was thinking about her operation. "Will getting my tonsils out hurt?" she asked me. "I'm really scared."

"Don't be scared, Lisa. Once your tonsils are out you'll feel much better. And in hospital you get as much ice-cream as you want."

"The worst part is, I'll be all alone." Her eyes filled with tears. "I missed you when you were away. I missed the boys, too. But I missed you the most."

I hugged her. She felt small and thin. "And I missed you," I told her. "Don't worry about the operation. You won't feel a thing. They'll put you to sleep, and when you wake up, we'll all be there. Janice and Joseph and the boys and me. Our whole family."

"Promise?" she asked.

"Everything's going to be all right, Kiddo. I promise."

---

operation (here) medical activity when doctors cut into a person's body to repair something

to braid [breɪd] to twist three strips of the hair at each side of the head into a single strip of hair

* * *

Showering took me longer now that I was working with horses. I tried to get home for a shower before the others so I wouldn't have to listen to their comments about the smell. The new bathroom was great. Janice and Joseph had surprised us with it when we got home from juvie.

My community service was cleaning out the *stalls* and brushing the police horses. I didn't mind the work, and I loved the horses. They were beginning to recognize me. I worked with a nice *First Nations* woman called Denise. I was lucky. I had the best job of all three of us.

Billy worked at the *recycling depot*, *sorting* glass, plastic, newspapers and *cardboard*. He came home dirty, too, but he didn't smell as bad as I did.

Tom's job was the worst. He had to scrub *pots* and *pans* in the kitchen at Burnaby General Hospital.

"Dirty, *smelly* pots," he complained when we were hanging out in the boys' room one night. "I hate it."

"You want to change jobs with me halfway

---

stall [stɔːl] →
First Nations Canadian description for the original inhabitants of Canada
recycling depot [riːˈsaɪklɪŋ‿ˈdepəʊ] place where re-usable items or materials (such as glass, cans etc.) are taken out of household rubbish
to sort to put things in groups according to type, size etc.
cardboard [ˈkɑːdbɔːd] very thick paper
smelly not smelling nice; having a bad smell

through?" asked Billy. "You'd love all that fresh air and *sunshine.*"

"You'd change jobs with me?"

"Sure thing. What are friends for?" He turned to me. "What's family for? Right, Nails?"

"Right. All for one and one for all," I grinned at him. "By the way, I've gone back to my real name. No more Nails, okay?"

Tom looked surprised. "No more Nails?"

"I like Nell," Billy said, smiling sweetly at me.

"Nell is a good name," said Tom thoughtfully. "My father used to say 'We learn little from victory, much more from *defeat*'."

I looked at Billy. Billy looked at me. "What's victory and defeat got to do with me changing my name back to Nell?"

Tom shrugged. "I'm not sure."

Billy laughed. Then I laughed, and Tom joined in.

After everything that had happened, I was ready for my real name. I'd been Nails long enough. It was time to be me again.

---

sunshine [ˈsʌnʃaɪn] light from the sun
defeat [dɪˈfiːt] opposite of 'victory'

Comprehension and activities

ONE

Activities

1. Who were the Three Musketeers? Write a short paragraph about them.
2. How much money (in Canadian dollars) did they rob from the bank? Find out how much this is in your own currency.
3. Find out something about Jane Austen and her novels. Several of them have been made into films or TV series. Perhaps you have even watched one!

Comprehension

1. Without reading the chapter again, describe the bank robbery in your own words.
2. What were Nell's feelings before and just after the robbery?
3. What are her feelings when she gets back home?
4. Why is Nell so exhausted at the end of the chapter?

Give your own opinion

1. At what point in the first chapter did you realize that the bank robbers were only in their early teens?
2. The normal motive for robbery is greed. Do you think this is why these three kids robbed the bank?
3. Do you think the robbery was well planned? Can you think of anything that could have gone wrong?
4. What do you think Nell means when she says: 'So much had changed in only one month'?

TWO

Activities

1. Why do some children need to go into foster homes? Make a list of possible reasons.

2. Try to imagine why each of the four children is in the Hardys' foster home.

Comprehension

1. What do we find out about any of the children's parents in this chapter?
2. What was different about the house on the day that Rhoda Mills came to inspect it?
3. How did Nell get her nickname?
4. Was Mrs. Osberg a good foster-mother? Say why or why not.
5. What will happen if Janice and Joseph can't comply with the new Social Services regulations?
6. What do you notice about the dialogues in this chapter? There are two interesting features (Janice/Joseph and Nell/Tom). What do they suggest?

Give your own opinion

1. How do you think Mrs. Osberg got her nickname?
2. Why do you think Mrs. Osberg became a foster mother?
3. Do you think the children have found a way of staying together?

THREE

Activities

1. Do you like gangster movies? Write down any that you have watched recently and discuss them with anybody who is reading the book with you.
2. If you don't like gangster movies, what kind of movies **do** you like?

Comprehension

1. Why does Tom agree with the new regulations about bathrooms?
2. Where does Billy get his idea for his plan from?
3. Why does Tom mention Robin Hood?
4. In what ways are Tom's and Nell's reactions to Billy's plan different?

5. What idea does Billy get from the way pickpockets work?

Give your own opinion

1. What sort of family background do you think Tom comes from?
2. Do you agree that stealing is for losers? Give your reasons.
3. Why do you think the authors put the first robbery into Chapter One instead of waiting until they had explained the situation?

FOUR

Activity

What are 'soaps' on TV and how did they get their name?

Comprehension

1. How does Nell get to False Creek?
2. What was Nell's family background?
3. How does Nell behave towards her mother?
4. What does Nell's mother do most of the day?
5. How did Nell think her mother could help her to raise some money?
6. What did Nell do after leaving her mother?

Give your own opinion

1. Would you have stolen the necklace if you had been Nell?
2. Should Nell have told her mother about her problems? Say why or why not.
3. What do you think is especially sad about Nell's mother's situation?

FIVE

Activity

For people in many English-speaking countries, the daffodil – one of the earliest spring flowers – is a symbol of new life after a long, cold winter. It is also the national flower of one of the four nations within the United Kingdom. Find out which one.

Comprehension

1. What message do the daffodils seem to be giving to Nell?
2. Explain in your own words what a trust fund is.
3. Why wasn't Tom able to get any money from his trust fund?
4. Describe in your own words how Billy plans to rob a bank.
5. What is wrong with his plan so far?

Give your own opinion

1. Why do you think Billy looks disappointed when Tom mentions getting money from the trust fund?
2. "Friggin' brainless I call it." Why do you think Tom's choice of the word 'brainless' might make Nell support Billy's bank-robbery plan more than Tom's criticism of it?
3. Do you think that Billy and Nell will manage to win Tom over to their plan? Give your reasons why or why not.

SIX

Activity

Billy says, "We're too young to go to prison." But he is not quite right.

The age at which children can be punished for a crime varies from country to country as well as from crime to crime. In Scotland it is 8 years old, in England, Wales and Northern Ireland it is 10, in Canada it is 12. Find out what the 'age of responsibility' is in your country and what happens to children below this age if they commit a crime.

Comprehension

1. Without reading the chapter again, write down what you know about Tom Okada. Then check the beginning of the chapter and add any extra information after your notes in a different colour ink.
2. What happened to Tom's dad after Tom's mother died?
3. What are Tom's arguments against the plan?
4. Why does he finally change his mind?

Give your own opinion

1. 'Okada' is not a typical Canadian surname. What nationality might Tom's father have been?
2. Why couldn't they tell Lisa about their plans?

SEVEN

Activities

Talk – or write – about the advantages and disadvantages of keeping a pet. Give at least five reasons for and five against, then draw your own personal conclusion.

Comprehension

1. Why might it not be a good idea for Lisa to have a pet?
2. What does Nell like most about her foster parents?
3. Why does Nell lose her appetite?
4. Without looking at the chapter again, write down what you can remember about Lisa's family background.

Give your own opinion

1. Why do you think Billy is on a high in this chapter?
2. What do you think Janice would do if Nell told her about Billy's plan to raise money?

EIGHT

Comprehension

1. What are the feelings of the Three Musketeers on the day after their first bank robbery?
2. What makes Nell so happy that day?
3. What sort of banks do they intend to rob?
4. Why does Nell tangle with Tom that evening?
5. What does this incident show?

Give your own opinion

1. Are there ever 'bathroom problems' in your family?
2. At the end of the chapter, Nell uses the words 'courteous', 'amiable' and 'despicable'. What sort of words are these?

NINE

Activities

Plan a bank robbery of your own! Write down all the details and discuss them with somebody. He or she may have useful suggestions! Is your plan foolproof?

Comprehension

1. Without reading the chapter again, describe the second bank job in your own words.
2. Describe the reactions of Nell, Tom and Billy to the failure of their second robbery.
3. What do these reactions tell you about their characters? Pick the most suitable adjective for each of the kids from this box:

> devil-may-care • happy-go-lucky • cautious
> daring • dog-in-a-manger • anxious
> terrified • scornful • extroverted
> hypocritical • blasé • introverted

If you are unsure of the meaning of any of these words, look them up in a dictionary.

Give your own opinion

1. Why do you think this second robbery was a failure?
2. What piece of bank-robbery 'equipment' might have stopped the young teller from screaming?

TEN

Comprehension

1. What happened to Tom when he started school?
2. Why couldn't Nails and Liesel help Tom?
3. How did Billy solve the problem?
4. In what way did Billy's actions influence Tom's participation in the bank robberies?

Give your own opinion

1. Is there – or was there – much bullying at your school?
2. What is, in your opinion, the best way to deal with bullying?
3. Where do you think Liesel Fischer's parents originally came from?

ELEVEN

Comprehension

1. Why does Billy dislike Tom's knuckle-cracking habit?
2. Compare the different feelings which Nell and Billy have during a robbery.
3. Why does Nell call Tom 'genius Tom'?
4. Has 'bank job number 3' been their most successful robbery yet?

Give your own opinion

1. Which of these words best matches Billy's statement about giving all banks the same chance of being robbed?
   POSITIVE - CYNICAL - IRONICAL - SARCASTIC
3. Why do you think Nell feels so bad about the success of the robbery?

TWELVE

Comprehension

1. What are the kids doing in the park?
2. Describe in your own words Nell's feelings in the park.
3. What are Joseph and Janice talking about when Nell gets back home?
4. Why can't Janice take a full-time job?
5. What is a mortgage?
6. Why does Nell count the money again?

Give your own opinion

1. Do you think the kids will manage to get the $10,000 they need?
2. How many more banks do you think they will need to rob?

THIRTEEN

Comprehension

1. Where were Nell and Tom waiting?
2. Why did Nell go into the bank?
3. How long did the bank job last – from start to finish?
4. Describe in your own words what happened after the robbery and before the police officer arrived.
5. Why did they have to let Billy go?
6. How does Billy persuade Tom to carry on with the robberies?

Give your own opinion

1. Why do you think the Three Musketeers are only robbing small banks?
2. If you were Tom, would you let Billy persuade you to carry on?

FOURTEEN

Comprehension

1. What change did Billy suggest in their method of operation?
2. What did the others think of his plan?
3. What was the best suggestion, and who made it?
4. What was Nell's conflict in this chapter?

Give your own opinion

1. Say why you think Billy's new method of operation would or wouldn't work.
2. Do you think that Tom's attitude towards the robberies is changing? Give your reasons.

FIFTEEN

Activities

This is bank job number five. Make a list of the five 'jobs' with the names of the banks and the amounts of money taken. Give each job a success rating in stars (zero to five). Are the Three Musketeers getting better or worse?

Comprehension

1. What did the kids do on Monday?
2. Describe the bank building in your own words.
3. What happened during the robbery?
4. Why did the girl in the bank start to cry?
5. What were the feelings of the Three Musketeers after this robbery?
6. What does Tom suggest that they do?

Give your own opinion

1. In what ways do you think the 'gang' is becoming more professional?
2. Do you think they could give the money back and ask the bank not to fire the girl?

SIXTEEN

Activity

Find out something about the 1950s cult film star James Dean.

Comprehension

1. Why did Janice want to talk to Nell before she went to school?
2. What did Janice ask Nell to buy?
3. What did Nell decide to buy instead?
4. Why couldn't Nell use the money from the shoe box to buy Billy's present?
5. What presents did Billy get?
6. Which present did he like best?

Give your own opinion

Why do you think that Nell didn't steal the coat?

SEVENTEEN

Activity

It always seems to be raining in Vancouver in April. What is the weather in British Columbia really like? Find out about it on the Internet.

Comprehension

1. What happened to Nell while Billy was robbing the bank?
2. What was ironical about this?
3. Where did Billy put his disguise and the money?
4. What happened to Nell next?
5. How did Nell get away?

Give your own opinion

1. The man from the bank can give a description of Nell to the police. Do you think it would have been better if she had not run away?
2. What could Nell have said to the police about the man?

EIGHTEEN

Activity

Find out how the city of Vancouver got its name.

Comprehension

1. Why was Nell surprised to hear that Billy had a father?
2. What is the difference between a hospital and a hospice?
3. What was wrong with Billy's dad?
4. Why did Billy take Nell to the hospice with him?
5. Was Billy angry at his dad?
6. Why didn't Billy get home until breakfast time on Monday?

Give your own opinion

1. What do you think might have happened to Billy's mother?
2. Why do you think that Billy's dad didn't wake up during their first visit?

NINETEEN

Activity

Think about the risks which Nell runs during each of the bank robberies. Make a list of them and describe Nell's reactions to each situation.

Comprehension

1. What sort of feeling did Nell have about this holdup and why?
2. What can you say about the man in the car?
3. Why was Nell angry with Tom?
4. Why did Tom say he was going to quit?
5. What was wrong when they got home?

Give your own opinion

1. Why do you think that Tom followed Nell home so closely?
2. What do you think will happen next?

TWENTY

Comprehension

1. Did they get a lot of money this time?
2. Who did Janice phone?
3. What was Janice's reaction when Nell showed her the money?
4. Why did Joseph get so angry?

Give your own opinion

1. Why do you think Janice didn't phone the police right away?
2. Have you ever skipped out of school? Did you have a good reason?
3. What do you think Joseph meant when he said: "You kids haven't thought this through very well"?

TWENTY-ONE

Comprehension

1. Describe the scene at the police station in your own words.
2. Did the police officers take them seriously at first?
3. Where did Officer Beckett take them?
4. Why did Officer Beckett have to fetch another chair?
5. How did the Chief Inspector treat the children?
6. Describe the contents of this chapter in your own words as briefly as you can.

Give your own opinion

1. Do you think that Billy might have been in trouble with the police before?
2. Nell asks herself: 'Why didn't they just arrest us and lock us up?' can you answer her question?

TWENTY-TWO

Comprehension

1. What can you say about the judge?
2. Who does Miss Farthingale criticize in court?
3. What was the punishment handed down by the judge?
4. What was the good news from the judge?
5. What were the feelings of the Three Musketeers at the end of the chapter?

TWENTY-THREE

Activity

Compare the treatment of young offenders in Canada and in your own country. How different is it?

Comprehension

1. Describe in your own words a typical day during Nell's month in juvie.
2. Why did some of the girls bully Nell?
3. How did Nell stop the bullying?
4. How were the two girls punished for fighting?
5. How were the two boys at the end of the month?

Give your own opinion

What sort of work do you think Billy and Tom would be doing?

TWENTY-FOUR

Activity

In Britain, community service is called 'Community Payback'. Find out more about this on the Internet. What sort of activities are involved in your country?

Comprehension

1. Why was Lisa scared?
2. What jobs did the three have to do as community service?
3. What was Janice and Joseph's surprise?
4. Why did Nell give up her nickname?

Find more exercises on
www.easyreaders.eu

Teen Reader Titles Now Available

English

Level 0
Philip Hewitt: Emma and the Boy Next Door (Sound)
Ann Halam: The Shadow on the Stairs

Level 1
Peter Johnson: Runaway Teacher
Alan Posener: The Double Life of a Very Black Cat
Stephen Speight: Bed & Breakfast (Sound)
Stephen Speight: The Runaway
Jeremy Taylor: Dr Schnitzler´s Dog
Jeremy Taylor: All 4 Love (Sound)
Wolf/Ferro: The Missing Mascot (Sound)

Level 2
Rita Bennet: The Scary Chat Room (Sound)
Kevin Brooks: Johnny Delgado – Private Detective
Annie Dalton: Friday Forever
Paul Davenport: Horror Trip on the Pecos River (Sound)
James Heneghan: Hit Squad
James Heneghan & Norma Charles: Bank Job
Philip Hewitt: Helping Hands
Philip Hewitt: Terror in the Hills
George Ivanoff: The Bookworm Mystery
Karen Mccombie: Love is the Drug
E. E. Richardsson: Black Bones
E. E. Richardsson: Devil for Sale (Sound)
Stephen Speight: The Fjord Murder (Sound)
Stephen Speight: Summer School Adventures
Andy Stanton: Sterling and the Canary
Jeremy Strong: Mad Iris
Jeremy Taylor: Football Friends (Sound)
Jeremy Taylor: Luke (Sound)
Lee Weatherly: Them

Level 3
Anne Cassidy: Talking to Strangers
Paul Davenport: A Matter of Principle
Paul Davenport: Crossroads to Love (Sound)
Paul Davenport: Wolf Watch
Paul Davenport: Snakeman
Charles Ferro: Horror at Remsen High
Charles Ferro: Moonstruck
Charles Ferro: Love Ties
Charles Ferro: Burning Love
Charles Ferro: The Fortune Teller
Charles Ferro: Kool-1
Charles Ferro: The Cave Mystery
Charles Ferro: Vampire Skeletons
Charles Ferro: Voodoo Zombies
Philip Hewitt: Quest for a Father
Sylvia Olsen: Yellow Line
Alan Posener: Oh! Carol and Other Steve Stories
Jeremy Taylor: Love me Blindly
Tony Varrato: Fakie

Level 4
Charles Ferro: Forever Young
Charles Ferro: Over the Line
Holly-Jane Rahlens: One Fine Day

German

Level 0
Iris Felter: Mädchen & Der Junge am Meer (Sound)
Greta Gallandy: Keine Angst? (Sound)
Patricia Mennen: Kopftuch

Level 1
Iris Felter: Tanz mit mir!
Greta Gallandy: Im Chatroom gefangen
Alan Posener: Kater, Ines und Katerina

Level 2
Alan Posener: Märchenland
Elsegret Ruge: Vier Freunde - Abenteuer in München (Sound)

Level 3
Alan Posener: Olli aus Ossiland

French

Level 0
Laurent Jouvet: Radio mystère (Sound)
Christiane Stéfanopoli:
Catastrophe au Camping des Roses (Sound)

Level 1
Michel Amelin: Cent vingt minutes pour mourir
Pascal Garnier: Les enfants de la nuit (Sound)
Lenia Major: La lettre mystérieuse
Brigitte Peskine: Mon grand petit frère (Sound)
Jérôme Talou: Parce que je t'aime

Level 2
Stéphane Daniel: Un agent trés secret
Anna Gavalda: 35 kilo d'espoir
Charlotte Gingras: Un été de Jade
Laurent Jouvet: Anne et l'ordinateur (Sound)
Laurent Jouvet: Répétition pour un crime
Jérôme Talou: L'amour par internet (Sound)
Paul Thiès: Un automne rouge sang (Sound)

Level 3
Michaël Ollivier: Frères de sang
Jérôme Talou: Bruno et l'amour

Level 4
Hallum/Louveau: Choc des cultures

Spanish

Level 0
Jaime Corpas: Amigos virtuales
Javier Navarro: Un mundo fantástico

Level 1
Jaime Corpas: Misterio en la Sagrada Familia
Javier Navarro: Una historia de montaña

Level 2
Javier Navarro: Las estátuas de Machu Picchu

Sound: Available as either Mp3 or CD,
check www.easyreaders.eu

Teen Reader Titles Now Available

Read On Series
English
Level 2 (A2) - including CD
Benni Bødker: Sarin in Sulphur Valley
Benni Bødker: Sarin in the Emperor's City
Benni Bødker: Sarin in the Foggy Mountains
Benni Bødker: Sarin in Nordheim
Benni Bødker: Sarin in the Salt Mine
Benni Bødker: Sarin and the star Tower

A-team Series
– Free MP3 available at www.easyreaders.eu
Level 3
Daniel Zimakoff & Ida-Marie Rendtorff: The Computer Mystery
Daniel Zimakoff & Ida-Marie Rendtorff: The Stolen Monkey
Daniel Zimakoff & Ida-Marie Rendtorff: Kidnapped

Labyrinth Series
German
Level 3 (A2/B1)
Martina Gattermann: Ein dramatischer Urlaub
(Sound available)
Martina Gattermann: SOS aus Wien
(Sound available)
Martina Gattermann: Horror in Hintertux
Martina Gattermann: Abenteuer in Berlin